Introduction

Future soccer superstar! You've got
maybe even a secret weapon of a l
mental grit to match? Let's be re
Beckham faced their moments. Imagine being the best
athlete in your whole country! That's exactly what happened to
Beckham in England. It started after the infamous red card in the
1998 World Cup. Think of how it must have felt: the pressure of
representing your country, the excitement of the World Cup stage,
and then the heart-wrenching moment when you make a split-
second mistake—kicking an opponent and earning a red card.

Suddenly, cheers turn into boos, and the entire nation is upset. The
media frenzy is like a storm, with every headline scrutinizing your
every move. Fans who once adored you are now calling for your
head, and imagine the weight of that disappointment not just from
the fans but also from your teammates and family. It's a crushing
moment, isn't it? But here's the fascinating part: Beckham didn't
let that define him.

Instead, he channeled that criticism into motivation, proving that
even the greatest can rebound from adversity. This book is about
building that same mental toughness so you can handle any
curveball life throws your way—just like Beckham. Are you
ready to learn how to rise above challenges and turn setbacks into
comebacks?

Now, let's imagine it's the final minute of the game, the score is
tied, and you're gearing up for that pivotal penalty kick. The

crowd is going wild, sweat's dripping down your face, and your heart's racing like it's in a sprint. In that high-stakes moment, how do you react? Do you falter under pressure, or do you clear your mind and focus? If you're aiming for greatness, it's gotta be option two, my friend.

Mental toughness is that secret ingredient that keeps you chill when others are losing it. It's all about staying focused, bouncing back from setbacks, and shaking off distractions. For all you soccer lovers, it's what separates sulking over a missed shot from shaking it off and playing even harder. It's like having a superpower that lets you stay upbeat no matter what challenges come your way. In soccer and life, it's the mentally tough who excel and rise to the top.

So why is mental toughness such a game-changer in soccer? Think of those nail-biting moments when the pressure skyrockets, your legs feel like jelly, and everyone's counting on you. A mentally tough player keeps their head in the game and delivers consistently, no matter how intense it gets. They don't just lean on their physical skills; they bring a rock-solid mindset that helps them play smarter, adapt quickly, and recover faster from mistakes. When the stakes are high, they shine the brightest, making crucial decisions that lead to victory. That's the power of mental toughness.

Now, let's dive into what's ahead in this book. We're going to explore loads of techniques and strategies that'll transform you into a mental powerhouse. You'll learn to set and smash realistic goals, become resilient when the going gets tough, and harness the magic of teamwork. We'll dig deep into mental tactics that give you the edge in any situation. By the time we wrap up, you won't just be a better athlete—you'll be unstoppable in whatever path you choose.

Being a young athlete isn't always a stroll in the park. There are highs and lows, triumphs and heartbreaks, pressures from coaches, expectations from parents, and sometimes, that sneaky self-doubt. This book gets what you're facing and aims to equip you with the tools to tackle these challenges head-on. Every young soccer player dreams of that glorious moment—scoring the winning goal, hearing the crowd erupt, feeling like a hero. But few recognize the mental hurdles on that journey. Our mission is to help you conquer those hurdles and emerge stronger, both on and off the field.

Let's be honest: playing sports is a blast, but it can be tough, too. Whether you're battling nerves before a big game, bouncing back from a tough loss, or striving to stay motivated during endless drills, it's not always a walkover. But guess what? Each challenge you face is a chance to bulk up that mental muscle. It's all part of the journey shaping you into not just a better player but a more confident and strong person.

So, what can you expect from this adventure? Imagine this book as your coach, leading you through the ins and outs of mental toughness. We'll kick off with the basics, like what mental toughness means and why it's your secret weapon. Then, we'll dive into setting goals that stick, staying positive under pressure, and bouncing back even stronger after setbacks. You'll also discover how teamwork can elevate your game.

But hold on, there's more (cue the infomercial voice)! We won't just talk about theories. This book is brimming with practical exercises, real-life stories, and enough humor to keep things lively—because learning should be fun, right? We'll learn how to weave these mental strategies into your everyday training and games, turning them into second nature.

By the end of this journey, you'll have a toolkit packed with mental tricks and life hacks, coupled with the confidence to use them. Whether it's handling criticism, staying calm under pressure, or picking yourself up after a tough game, you'll be ready for it all. And the best part? The perks of mental toughness reach far beyond the soccer field. These skills will help you excel in school, friendships, and whatever future you carve out.

We know being a young athlete feels like juggling a million tasks at once. There are glorious moments and times you'd rather forget. Coaches will push you, family might have sky-high expectations, and don't get me started on your inner critic. But trust me, this book gets it, and it's packed with everything you need to face these challenges head-on.

Every soccer player dreams of that epic moment—the game-winning goal, the thunderous cheers, the rush of victory. But few foresee the mental hurdles along the way. We're here to help you not just leap over those hurdles but bulldoze right through them, coming out even stronger and more resilient, both on and off the pitch.

Now, let's be real: sports are exhilarating, but they're also demanding. Pre-game jitters, post-loss blues, and endless drills—it's all part of the game. Yet every hurdle, every setback, is a chance to flex that mental muscle. This journey will mold you into not just an exceptional player but a confident and tenacious individual.

So, what's in store for our adventure? Think about this book as your trusty sidekick, showing you the ropes of mental toughness.

We'll unravel what it means, why it matters, and how to harness it, from setting unbeatable goals to staying cool under pressure and bouncing back stronger than ever.

And hey, we're not stopping at theories. Expect hands-on exercises, relatable stories, and enough humor to keep you entertained. We'll embed these strategies deep into your routines until they become second nature.

Soon, you'll wield a toolbox filled with mental tactics and life hacks supported by unshakeable confidence. Whether it's facing criticism, keeping cool amidst chaos, or recovering from losses, you'll be ready. Plus, mental toughness doesn't just ace soccer— it powers success in school, friendships, and whatever future you create.

Ready to dive in? Let's embark on this thrilling journey and tap into the mental strength within. Cheers to becoming not just a fierce athlete but an extraordinary person. Game on!

CHAPTER 1

Mental Toughness

I'm more worried about being a good person than being the best football player in the world. –Lionel Messi

Ethan sat on the bench, watching his teammates hustle on the field. He felt that familiar knot in his stomach, the kind he experienced before important games. "You can do this," he told himself, trying to drown out the doubts creeping into his mind. His coach walked over, noticing the uneasy look on his face. "Hey, you've trained hard for this," Coach Peters said, sitting down beside him. "Remember, it's all about your mindset. Focus on what you can control." Ethan nodded. He had read about the importance of mental toughness, but putting it into practice was another challenge entirely.

Ethan stood at the field edge, adrenaline coursing through him as the final game began. Each whistle, each pass, everything at that moment mattered. With anticipation buzzing in the air, he lifted his chin and stepped into the action, ready to put everything he learned to the ultimate test. He felt the mental muscles flexing, prepared to not only play a game but to perform with grace under pressure.

Understanding mental toughness is important for every young soccer player. It's not about being a robot or invincible but having that inner strength to manage stress, remain confident, and keep your eyes on the prize no matter what.

In this chapter, we'll delve into the nitty-gritty of mental toughness and why it's a game-changer in soccer. We'll explore essential traits such as resilience, focus, confidence, and stress management. You'll learn how bouncing back like a rubber band after setbacks can make you unstoppable. We'll discuss staying laser-focused even when the stadium turns into a circus of distractions. Confidence will be another highlight—believing in yourself and taking those daring shots because you trust your skills. We'll also touch on practical ways to keep calm under pressure, making sure anxiety doesn't sabotage your performance. Get ready to discover these powerful mental tools and how to sharpen them to elevate your game!

What Is Mental Toughness?

Mental toughness is super important for soccer players, and it's not just about being physically strong or able to run for miles without getting tired. It's made up of a bunch of different traits, like resilience, focus, confidence, and the ability to manage stress. Let's break that down a bit.

Bouncing Back

Resilience is the ability to bounce back from setbacks, whether that's losing a match or missing an important goal. Think of it like being a rubber band—you might get stretched out of shape, but you snap right back. This trait helps you keep going even when things are tough, and it's essential for any athlete who wants to succeed in the long run.

Focus

Focus is all about keeping your eye on the prize. In soccer, this means not getting distracted by the crowd, the other team, or even your own mistakes. Staying focused helps you make smart decisions on the field and keeps you in the game mentally, even when things are going haywire.

Confidence

Confidence is knowing you can do it, even when the odds are against you. It's believing in your skills and your training, and it shows in how you play. A confident player takes risks, like going for that tricky shot or making a bold pass, because they trust themselves. Without confidence, even the most talented players can hesitate and miss opportunities.

Handling Stress

Then there's the ability to manage stress. Soccer can be super stressful, with high stakes and lots of pressure. Being able to stay calm and composed, even in the heat of the moment, is crucial. This means finding ways to relax and not let anxiety take over so you can perform at your best.

Understanding these characteristics will also help you see where your strengths lie and what needs a bit more work. Maybe you've got resilience down pat—you never let a loss get you down—but you could use a bit more focus during games. Or perhaps you're good at managing stress but need to build more confidence in your abilities.

Building Mental Toughness

So, how do you go about building mental toughness? Well, it starts with small, everyday practices. For example, setting short-term goals can help build confidence as you achieve them one by one. Visualization techniques can improve focus—imagine yourself making that perfect pass or scoring that goal. Stress management can involve simple things like deep-breathing exercises or positive self-talk.

Listen to Feedback

Taking feedback positively is another important aspect. Sometimes criticism can sting, but viewing it as a chance to get better can make a world of difference. If a coach tells you that you need to work on your passing accuracy, don't take it as an insult; take it as valuable advice to improve your game.

Rise to Challenges

Another way to build mental toughness is by facing challenges head-on. When you encounter tough situations in games or practices, instead of shying away, embrace them. See them as opportunities to test your mental strength and grow stronger. Over time, this attitude will help you become more resilient and better at handling whatever comes your way.

Be a Team Player

Team dynamics also play a role in building mental toughness. Being part of a supportive team can boost your confidence and help you manage stress. When you know your teammates have your back, it's easier to take risks and push yourself. So, focus on building good relationships with your teammates and fostering a positive team culture.

Learn From Your Mistakes

Lastly, remember that everyone has bad days. Even the best players in the world miss shots, make mistakes, and lose games. What sets them apart is how they bounce back. So, if you mess up, don't dwell on it. Learn from it and move on. Each setback is just a stepping stone on your path to becoming mentally tougher.

Why Mental Toughness Is Important

Think about those nail-biting moments in a match where everything's on the line. An athlete with mental toughness isn't fazed by the crowd, the scoreboard, or the ticking clock. They've trained not just physically but mentally to handle these high-stress situations. It's like they have an internal switch that they can flip to stay calm and focused. This ability to perform under pressure consistently leads to better outcomes when it matters.

Now, let's talk about bouncing back from challenges. In competitive sports, failures are inevitable—you miss a goal, you lose a game, and you get injured. Athletes with mental toughness don't let these setbacks define them. Instead, they view challenges as obstacles to overcome, not roadblocks. They push through pain and fatigue, knowing that persistence is key to success. This not only boosts their performance but also helps foster a growth mindset, which is essential for both personal and team development.

It's important to note that mental toughness doesn't mean never showing emotion. There's a huge misconception that being mentally tough means acting like a robot devoid of any feelings. The truth is mentally tough athletes do experience fear, anxiety, and even doubt. The difference is they don't let these emotions control their actions. They acknowledge their feelings and then refocus on their goals (Admin, 2020). This kind of emotional intelligence is crucial because it allows them to navigate both the highs and lows of sports and life effectively.

11

Moreover, mental toughness extends beyond the soccer field. Athletes who develop resilience and a positive mindset often find these skills useful in other areas of their lives. Whether it's handling the pressure of exams, dealing with personal issues, or managing stress at work, the principles of mental toughness apply universally. It's like having a secret superpower that helps you tackle life's challenges head-on.

Tips for Building Your Mental Toughness

There are several strategies athletes can use to build mental toughness:

- Visualization techniques can help, where players imagine themselves succeeding in various scenarios.
- Mindfulness practices, such as meditation, can teach them how to stay present and focused.
- Positive self-talk is another valuable tool. Instead of letting negative thoughts take over, mentally tough athletes remind themselves of their strengths and past successes.

These techniques combined create a solid foundation upon which mental toughness is built.

One more thing to keep in mind is that mental toughness isn't about being perfect. No one performs flawlessly all the time. What matters is how you respond to mistakes and setbacks. The ability to quickly recover from a misstep and focus on the next play is a hallmark of mental toughness. It's about maintaining composure, staying determined, and keeping the end goal in sight.

Mental Toughness in Soccer

When you're on the soccer field, it's not just your physical skills that are being tested—it's your mental strength, too. Mental toughness plays a significant role in how well you handle high-pressure situations, make quick decisions, and execute your moves effectively. Let's explore this concept further and see how it directly impacts your soccer performance.

Benefits of Mental Toughness for Your Soccer Performance

First off, soccer is full of high-pressure moments. Whether it's making the winning pass in the final seconds or taking a critical penalty kick, these situations demand mental toughness. It helps you stay calm and composed, allowing you to perform at your best, even when the stakes are high. When you're mentally tough, you view pressure as a challenge rather than a threat, giving you a competitive edge over your opponents.

Fun Fact:

Cristiano Ronaldo is the all-time top scorer in UEFA Champions League history, with over 140 goals!

Did you know?

Ronaldo is obsessed with training so much that he once took a gym break during a photoshoot and returned so sweaty the makeup team had to fix him up!

Making Decisions

In soccer, you often have only a split second to decide whether to pass, shoot, or dribble. Mental toughness influences these rapid-fire decisions by enabling you to analyze situations more clearly and make choices confidently. Mentally tough players remain focused and attentive, ensuring they select the best possible action, even when under immense stress. This sharpness can be the difference between scoring a goal and losing possession.

On Target

Imagine attempting a complex maneuver like a bicycle kick. If you let nerves get the better of you, your chance of pulling it off diminishes. However, with strong mental skills, you can concentrate fully on the technique, blocking out any distractions and enhancing your execution. Mental toughness helps maintain high levels of accuracy and precision, regardless of external pressures.

Mental Stamina

You might have the stamina to run for 90 minutes and the agility to dodge defenders, but without mental toughness, these physical attributes can only take you so far. True completeness as an athlete comes from the synergy of both mental and physical training. Think of top players like Lionel Messi or Cristiano Ronaldo; their success isn't just due to their physical prowess but also their unshakeable mental strength.

Keep Calm

When players can stay calm and collected, they're more likely to score that winning goal or defend against an attack effectively. It's all about keeping those nerves in check and executing plays just like you practiced. According to the folks at Elite Football Coaching Sydney, handling high-pressure situations by staying mentally strong directly impacts decision-making and performance during critical moments (David, 2024).

Smooth Recovery

Let's face it: everyone messes up sometimes, but the trick is not letting it get to you. If you miss a shot or fumble a pass—it is no big deal. Instead of beating yourself up over it, mental toughness helps you shake it off and focus on the next play. This way, one mistake doesn't spiral into a bad game. By rebounding quickly, you can maintain your confidence and even learn from those little slip-ups to come back stronger than before.

Laser Focus

In soccer, distractions are everywhere—loud stadiums, distracting opponents, and your racing thoughts. But guess what? Mental toughness acts like blinders, helping you block out all that noise. With rock-solid focus, you can stick to your game plan and deliver a consistently strong performance. Think of it like having tunnel vision where the only thing that matters is the game right in front of you. This level of concentration ensures you're always in the right place at the right time, ready to make impactful decisions.

Team Player

Your ability to stay positive and resilient can uplift your teammates, boosting their morale and improving overall team cohesion. Let's say you're the captain—your mental resilience can inspire others to keep pushing even when things look bleak. This unity and shared determination can create a stronger, more motivated team that performs better together.

Strengthening Your Mind

There are a few great strategies you can start adopting into your daily life that will help you along your journey to turning your mind into a mental powerhouse. Let's look at some of them together.

Visualization

One effective technique is visualization. Picture yourself nailing that penalty kick or making that crucial save. The more you visualize success, the more confident and prepared you'll feel in real-life scenarios. Visualization helps program your brain to perform under stress, almost like muscle memory, but for your mind.

Set Goals

Goal setting is another essential tool. Set clear, achievable goals, both short-term and long-term. Maybe it's scoring a certain number of goals this season or improving your passing accuracy. These targets give you something concrete to strive for, keeping you motivated and focused. Make sure to celebrate small victories along the way; this keeps your morale high and reaffirms your progress.

Mindfulness

Mindfulness and relaxation techniques can also be game-changers. Practices like deep breathing exercises, mindfulness meditation, or progressive muscle relaxation can help you manage stress and keep your composure. Including these routines in your daily life can build a more resilient mindset, making you less vulnerable to anxiety during matches.

Positive Self-Talk

Positive self-talk is key, too. We all have that inner voice, and if yours tends to be a bit of a downer, it's time to change the script. Replace negative thoughts with uplifting affirmations. Tell yourself you're capable, you're prepared, and you've got this. This shift in mindset can boost your confidence and reduce performance anxiety.

Having Support

Don't forget the power of support. Talking to coaches, sports psychologists, or trusted teammates can provide valuable perspective and reassurance. Sharing your experiences and challenges helps you feel less isolated and more equipped to tackle mental barriers.

Wrap it Up!

Alright, now that you've got a solid grip on mental toughness and its role in soccer, it's time to put it all into practice. Remember, being mentally tough isn't just about handling stressful game moments; it's about bouncing back from mistakes, staying focused amid chaos, and keeping your cool no matter what. Whether you're nailing that last-minute goal or brushing off a missed shot, these skills will make you a stronger player on and off the field.

And don't forget, mental toughness is like a muscle—the more you train it, the stronger it gets. Visualize your success, set achievable goals, and keep a positive inner dialogue. Plus, lean on your teammates for support; their belief in you can boost your confidence and motivation. So, go out there, embrace every challenge, and show the world that not only can you kick a ball, but you can also handle anything life throws your way with grace and grit!

Setting goals and staying motivated are like peanut butter and jelly for young soccer athletes. They're both important elements that make the experience not only bearable but also fun. In the next chapter, we'll be diving headfirst into these important skills, so stay tuned!

CHAPTER 2

Keeping Your Eyes on the Prize

Life is like soccer; you need goals. –Anonymous

Liam was a promising young soccer player who played for his local club, the Greenfield Warriors. He had a natural talent for the game, but he often struggled with consistency, especially during crucial matches. One foggy Saturday morning, after a frustrating loss where he missed two penalty shots, he sat down with his coach, Matt. "I just don't know how to get better," he sighed, running his fingers through his tousled hair. Coach Matt looked him in the eye. "Liam, it's all about setting some specific goals. Let's break down what you want to achieve."

As they talked, Coach Matt encouraged Liam to think about where he wanted to be by the end of the season. "What if you set a goal to improve your penalty kicks by 30%?" he suggested. "And how about tracking your weekly progress? You can practice penalties with a buddy and record how many you score out of ten." Liam felt the determination bubbling inside him. "Okay! That sounds doable," he replied enthusiastically. "What else can I do?"

Without clear goals, you might feel like you're kicking a ball around in random directions, hoping it ends up in the net by sheer luck. And let's face it, luck isn't going to help you when you're one-on-one with the goalie in the final match of the season. So, getting your goal-setting game strong is like putting on your shin guards—necessary protection against the chaos of aimless wandering.

In this chapter, we're diving into the nitty-gritty of setting effective goals and maintaining that ever-elusive thing called motivation. You'll uncover techniques that can transform your vague dreams into concrete targets, making it easier to plot your course toward soccer greatness. We'll also explore strategies to keep your fire burning, even when training sessions start to feel like watching paint dry. From learning how to tailor your objectives to ensure they push you closer to your ultimate dreams to discovering tricks for keeping your spirits high, this chapter has all the tools you need to elevate your game. Enjoy the journey of turning your aspirations into achievements and transforming hard work into habitual success.

How to Set SMART Goals

When it comes to setting goals in soccer, or any sport for that matter, it can make all the difference between just playing and truly excelling. So, what kind of goals are we talking about? We're talking SMART goals:

- specific
- measurable
- achievable
- relevant
- time-bound

This approach is essential for young athletes because it provides clarity and direction.

Specific

First off, let's dive into the importance of being specific with your goals. Imagine saying, "I want to be better at soccer." Sure, it's a noble idea, but it's way too broad and vague. It leaves you wondering where to start and what exactly you need to work on. Instead, say something like, "I want to increase my passing accuracy by 20%." Now that's specific! This kind of goal gives you a clear target to aim for. You know exactly what aspect of your game needs improvement and how to measure your progress.

Measurable

If you can't measure your goals, how do you even know if you're getting better? Let's stick with our passing accuracy example. Track your passes during practice and games. How many successful passes are you making out of every 10? By keeping count, you have tangible evidence of your improvement. And when you see those numbers go up, it's incredibly rewarding. Plus, if things aren't progressing as planned, these measurements give you the insight needed to adjust your training methods.

Achievable

We all love to dream big, but setting super-ambitious goals can sometimes do more harm than good. Let's say you're aiming to become the top scorer in your league this season. While it's great to aim high, you also need to ask yourself if it's realistic, given your current skills and competition level. A more achievable goal might be to improve your scoring rate by, let's say, making at least one goal per game. This keeps the challenge manageable and helps build your confidence along the way. Balance is key here; the goal should challenge you but also be within reach.

Relevant

Your goals should align with your broader aspirations. For instance, if your ultimate dream is to become an elite defender, then improving your passing accuracy is relevant. However, focusing too heavily on scoring goals might not be as pertinent.

Make sure each goal takes you a step closer to your long-term ambitions.

Time-Bound

Time-bound objectives add a layer of urgency and focus. If you say, "I will increase my passing accuracy by 20% within three months," you've given yourself a clear deadline. This helps you stay disciplined and committed to your training schedule.

One last thing: Life happens. Sometimes, things don't go according to plan. Maybe you got injured or encountered some other obstacle. That's okay. The beautiful thing about SMART goals is their flexibility. If you find that a goal isn't working out as expected, you can always reassess and adjust it. Just remember to keep it specific, measurable, achievable, relevant, and time-bound.

So there you have it. Setting SMART goals might sound a bit too structured or even boring initially, but trust me, it works wonders. Whether you're looking to up your game in passing, shooting, or overall fitness, having a clear road map will help you get there faster and with less frustration. Start with one area you want to improve, set a SMART goal, and watch as your performance elevates. And hey, not only does this make practice more effective, but checking off those goals feels pretty darn good, too. Happy goal-setting, future soccer stars!

Tips for Staying Motivated

Let's be honest here; there are days when motivation feels out of reach. Some mornings, you might wake up excited to tackle your goals, ready to give it your all. On other days, you may just want to lounge on the couch and binge-watch your favorite Netflix series. But staying consistent is crucial for success. The question is: How can you maintain that drive on the days when it's hard to find? Here are some tips that you can try to keep your motivation levels up even when the going gets tough.

Creating a Routine

When it comes to achieving goals, having a routine can make a significant difference. Think about the last time you tried to improve at something, like playing soccer. If you jumped into practice without a set plan, you might have felt lost, as if you were running in circles without direction. Establishing a routine helps create consistency in your practice.

Setting aside specific times each day for your training can help you form a habit. When practice is scheduled, it becomes easier to show up regularly, even on those days when motivation is lacking. For instance, you might decide to train for thirty minutes every weekday after school. This steadiness not only ensures you are improving but also helps instill a sense of discipline. Over time, what may initially feel like a chore can become a normal part of your day.

Celebrating Small Wins

Acknowledging small victories is more important than many realize. When you notice and celebrate these tiny milestones, you create feelings of accomplishment and joy that can boost your motivation. Think about it: Did you just achieve a personal best in juggling the ball? Write it down or create a chart to keep track of these achievements.

Visual reminders can be incredibly impactful. You might find that simply seeing your progress laid out in front of you can be a huge motivator on days when motivation is hard to find. Creating a system of tracking your small wins can keep you energized and push you forward. Every little win adds up, and before you know it, those small victories can lead to bigger successes.

Make It Fun

Finding the right balance in practice can sometimes feel challenging, but it's crucial to maintain your enthusiasm. Incorporating lighthearted drills and enjoyable activities can transform your training from a chore into an exciting experience. Do you remember the thrill of simply playing soccer with friends? That pure enjoyment is what you should strive to recapture. To reignite that excitement, combine your training sessions with activities that genuinely inspire you.

Think about adding some games to your practice routine. Instead of adhering strictly to conventional drills, consider introducing playful challenges. For instance, dedicate one day to enhancing your dribbling by organizing a fun race with teammates. On another occasion, focus on improving your shooting precision through a friendly contest. Mixing up your training keeps it engaging and allows you to build a variety of skills effectively.

Accountability Buddies

An effective way to stay motivated is to find someone who can support and hold you accountable. This person could be a coach, a teammate, or even a close friend. Having someone who knows your goals and progress can create a sense of responsibility. When you tell someone about your intentions, it becomes harder to let yourself off the hook.

This sense of accountability can push you to show up and do your best, knowing someone else is rooting for you. Plus, having someone to share your journey with can make the entire experience more enjoyable. You can share struggles, encourage each other, and celebrate achievements together.

Keep It Personal

Every athlete is unique and driven by different motives. Some thrive on competition, while others are excited by learning new skills. By personalizing your training approach, you can ensure that your sessions align with your motivations. For example, if you are someone who loves competing, you might want to set up friendly challenges with a teammate.

If you are more interested in skill development, consider treating yourself to mastering one new trick each week. This tailoring of your strategies can keep you engaged and provide the excitement needed to approach practice with enthusiasm. When training reflects your interests, it can turn into something you genuinely look forward to.

Stay Balanced

Finding the right balance is essential. Too much practice without adequate rest can lead to burnout. When you overtrain, it might leave you feeling drained, both physically and mentally. Additionally, it might also drain your motivation. It's important to schedule time for recovery and engage in activities outside of your sport.

Consider taking up yoga for relaxation or set aside weekends to spend time with friends. Balancing intense training with fun and relaxation can help maintain your energy levels in both your mind and body. When you feel rejuvenated, you will come back to practice with renewed vigor and enthusiasm, ready to tackle challenges head-on.

Self-Reflection

Self-reflection is a powerful motivator that many people overlook. Taking time to think about your progress and feelings can provide clarity and drive. Keeping a journal where you jot down thoughts, feelings, and observations about your performance can be incredibly helpful.

By documenting your journey, you can recognize accomplishments and pinpoint areas that need improvement. Moreover, regular self-reflection meetings—either with yourself or a coach—can provide you with valuable insights. This practice acts like a personal motivational pep talk, constantly reminding you of your aspirations and helping you find your direction. It's a space to appreciate how far you've come while setting your sights on where you want to go next.

Fun Fact:

In a Bundesliga match against Wolfsburg in 2015, Robert Lewandowski scored five goals in just nine minutes after coming on as a substitute, setting multiple records, including the fastest hat-trick in Bundesliga history.

Did you know?

Lewandowski holds a black belt in karate, a skill he credits for helping his balance and agility on the field. He practiced karate during his younger years before fully committing to soccer.

Be Inspired

Role models can offer a powerful source of inspiration. Study the journeys of professional athletes whose paths you admire. Notice their dedication, hard work, and the obstacles they've overcome. Knowing that even the best have faced struggles can motivate you to push through your challenges.

Let's dive into the inspiring journeys of some renowned soccer players who have incredibly set and pursued their goals, showcasing how determination and a clear vision can lead to tremendous success.

Cristiano Ronaldo

Cristiano Ronaldo's extraordinary dedication to training has made him an icon in the soccer world. Ronaldo's journey began on the small Portuguese island of Madeira, where he honed his skills day in and day out. What sets Ronaldo apart is his obsessive pursuit of excellence. Even now, after achieving immense success, his training regimen remains intense and unwavering.

Ronaldo wakes up early and follows a rigorous schedule that includes strength training, cardiovascular workouts, and technical drills. His commitment to physical fitness is unparalleled, often going beyond what is required by his clubs. This dedication showcases the importance of setting high standards and continually pushing oneself to achieve them. Ronaldo's work ethic serves as a powerful reminder that even the most talented athletes need discipline and hard work to maintain their elite status.

Megan Rapinoe

Megan Rapinoe's goal-setting process is unique because it involves both her career and her activism. On the field, Rapinoe has always set high standards for herself, aiming to be the best and win major tournaments. Off the field, she focuses on creating opportunities and fighting for justice. Her advocacy for growth emphasizes that dedicated athletes can have a broader impact beyond sports. Rapinoe's story encourages young athletes to pursue their dreams while also contributing positively to the community.

Kylian Mbappé

Kylian Mbappé's rise to prominence is a testament to the power of clear goal-setting. Mbappé grew up in Bondy, a suburb of Paris, where he quickly stood out for his speed and skill on the soccer field. From a young age, Mbappé had a focused vision of becoming a professional soccer player. His family supported his ambitions, providing the necessary environment for him to thrive.

Mbappé joined AS Monaco's youth academy and soon made his mark, debuting for the first team at just 16. His performance was so impressive that it caught the attention of major European clubs. His focused vision and specific goals helped fuel his rapid ascent in the soccer world. Moving to Paris Saint-Germain (PSG) and playing alongside some of the world's best players further accelerated his development. Mbappé's story illustrates that with tenacity and a clear plan, young athletes can turn their dreams into reality.

These real-life examples show that effective goal-setting and maintaining motivation are crucial for achieving success in soccer or any other field. Whether it's Ronaldo's dedication, Rapinoe's advocacy, or Mbappé's focused vision, there is something to learn from each of these athletes.

Wrap it Up!

So there you have it, young soccer stars! We've talked about how to set those SMART goals to keep you focused and motivated. Whether it's nailing down what exactly you want to improve, making sure you can track your progress, ensuring your goals are achievable and relevant, or giving yourself a clear deadline, these steps are your road map to success. Remember, being specific helps you know exactly what you're aiming for, while keeping things measurable lets you see how far you've come. And hey, setting realistic goals means you're challenging yourself just enough without setting yourself up for disappointment.

Now, let's not forget the importance of sticking to your routines and celebrating those small wins. It's easy to get bogged down in the grind, but mixing in some fun keeps your passion alive. Having an accountability buddy can give you that extra push, and personalizing your motivation strategies ensures you stay pumped up. Keep your training varied to avoid monotony, and make sure to balance work with some playtime to prevent burnout. By incorporating these techniques into your daily practice, you're well on your way to becoming not just a better soccer player but also a more mentally tough athlete. Go out there, set those goals, and start kicking toward your dreams!

Confidence isn't about showing off or being the loudest player out there; it's about believing in your abilities and trusting that all the hard work you put in will pay off. In the next chapter, we'll be looking at ways for you to boost your confidence and become the best player you can be! Let's go!

CHAPTER 3

The Key to Confidence

*It doesn't matter if I have bad luck. I keep going, and at the end
of the day, I'll always get my reward*–Robert Lewandowski

Lionel Messi faced a huge challenge in his early years. As a kid,
he was shorter than most of his friends, which often put him in the
background during games. Coaches sometimes overlooked him
solely because of his height. It was tough, but instead of
succumbing to doubt, Messi decided to trust himself. He
dedicated countless hours to practice, perfecting his skills. Every
kick of the ball felt like a step closer to his dreams. He often
reminded himself, "What matters is the size of my heart," a
mantra that guided him through tough times.

Messi's path was filled with bumps. At 13, he moved to
Barcelona, leaving behind everything he knew in Argentina.
Alone and separated from his family, he felt the heavy burden of
uncertainty. The pressure was intense. One night, after a grueling
training session, he contemplated giving up. Sitting alone in his
room, he whispered encouraging words to himself. "You belong
here," he assured himself, fighting back tears. The next day, he
entered the field with renewed determination, viewing every
challenge as a chance to elevate himself.

Training became a platform for self-discovery. He didn't see
crucial games as mere tests; instead, he viewed them as
opportunities for growth. Each goal he netted filled him with
newfound confidence. He once said, "I'm not scared of making
mistakes; I'm scared of not trying." This perspective propelled his

development. Mistakes transformed into valuable lessons, and every setback pushed him to strive even harder.

As he moved up to the first team, new hurdles emerged. The entire world had its eyes on him. In his first match, the weight of expectation loomed large. Just before stepping onto the pitch, he took a deep breath and reminded himself, "You've trained for this moment." When the whistle blew, he chose to enjoy the game rather than dwell on fear. The first touch felt incredible, reinforcing his belief that he was exactly where he was meant to be.

Each match brought fresh challenges and scrutiny. There were times when he missed easy shots or faced off against tougher opponents. Instead of letting those instances define him, he visualized success. After a tough game, he replayed his mistakes in his mind and imagined himself conquering those challenges. Each visualization strengthened his resolve. "Visualize it," he'd tell himself. "You've got this."

In discussions with his teammates, Messi emphasized the power of self-confidence. "Confidence isn't about showing off," he explained. "It's about trusting your skills." His humility shone through, and his teammates drew inspiration from such conversations. They appreciated how Messi openly shared his fears alongside his successes.

As Messi's career progressed, he made it a point to share his experiences. Frequently speaking at youth camps, he taught young players about the importance of self-belief. "Every superstar has wrestled with self-doubt," he would share, making the journey relatable. He encouraged kids to confront their anxieties. Setbacks are simply stepping stones toward success;

there's no shame in stumbling; what matters is the resilience to rise again.

His story made a significant impact. Young soccer players would approach him, eager to absorb his wisdom. In these moments, he always redirected the conversation to mindset and confidence. "Believe in yourself and work hard," he advised. His words inspired not just budding athletes but everyone who heard them, reminding them that perseverance and hard work are the foundations of confidence.

As the years passed, Messi collected numerous awards and accolades but never lost sight of how crucial confidence was in his journey. There were moments of self-doubt, even in his brightest days, but he acknowledged them and reaffirmed his trust in himself. He practiced affirmations daily and continuously visualized his goals. His relentless efforts shaped not only his career but also his character.

Reflecting on his achievements, he often shared a thought that resonated deeply: "Every goal I scored began as just an idea. When you believe in yourself, those ideas can become real." His words conveyed a universal truth: Victory stems from unwavering belief. It's a lesson that applies far beyond soccer and is relevant to every aspect of life.

This chapter is packed with practical exercises and strategies designed specifically to help you build that unshakeable confidence. Whether it's through daily affirmations or visualization techniques, these tools are all geared toward making you feel like a champion before you even step foot on the field.

We also explore how to embrace feedback and turn setbacks into comebacks, fostering a mindset of growth rather than fear. You'll learn to squash negative self-talk and replace it with positive reinforcement, helping you stay mentally strong during games and practices. By the end of this chapter, you'll have a toolkit full of confidence-boosting exercises that will not only improve your performance on the soccer field but also spill over into other areas of your life. Get ready to unlock the best version of yourself and face each match with an unbreakable spirit!

Fun Fact:

José Mourinho has won league titles in four different countries—Portugal, England, Italy, and Spain—making him one of the most successful managers in the world!

Did you know?

Mourinho once hid in a laundry basket to sneak into his team's locker room during a Champions League match while he was banned from the sideline!

Daily Confidence-Building Exercises

Building confidence is a game-changer on and off the soccer field. It's like having a secret superpower that helps you tackle any challenge head-on. Let's dive into some exercises that can be part of your daily routines to boost self-confidence and improve performance.

Hype Yourself

One fantastic way to start is by keeping a journal for daily affirmations. You know those days when everything feels like it's going wrong? That's when a positivity boost comes in handy.

Writing down affirmations such as "I am strong," "I am capable," or even "I rocked that last practice" can make a world of difference. These positive statements help create a positive self-image, almost like giving your mind high-fives every morning! Plus, it's a great habit to look back at how far you've come.

Get Feedback

Constructive feedback isn't just about pointing out mistakes; it's a gold mine of growth opportunities. Seek advice from coaches, teammates, and even friends who understand the game. Feedback helps athletes identify areas for improvement and focus on growth rather than shortcomings. Instead of fearing criticism, use it as a tool for becoming better. For example, if a coach points out that you need to work on your stamina, incorporate more endurance exercises into your routine. Viewing feedback as a stepping stone rather than a stumbling block makes all the difference.

Incorporating these practices into daily routines isn't just about immediate gains but long-term development. Affirmation journaling instills a positive mindset, visualization prepares the mind, setting small challenges ensures steady progress, and seeking feedback fosters continuous improvement. Confidence doesn't sprout overnight, but with these consistent efforts, young athletes will find themselves growing stronger and more assured in their abilities.

How to Overcome Self-Doubt

Alright, let's dive into building confidence on the soccer field by handling self-doubt like champs.

Kick Negative Thoughts to the Curb

First off, let's tackle negative self-talk head-on. Ever caught yourself thinking, "I can't do this" or "I'm just not good enough"? That's self-doubt creeping in. The more we entertain these thoughts, the bigger they grow. To squash them, it's important to recognize when they pop up. Next time you hear that inner critic, challenge it! Instead of saying, "I'm going to mess up," flip it around to, "I've got this." Even if you don't believe it 100% at first, fake it till you make it. With practice, positive self-talk can become second nature.

Pick the Right Squad

Now, let's talk about your squad outside the field. Having a solid support network is like having a secret weapon against self-doubt. Surround yourself with positive vibes from friends, family, and coaches who believe in you. When you're feeling down or doubting yourself, lean on them for support. Sometimes, all it takes is a pep talk from a friend or some encouraging words from a coach to remind you of your strengths.

Stay Grounded

Coping strategies are another game-changer. Let's say you're feeling jittery before a big match. What do you do? Breathing techniques can be your best friend here. Try taking deep, slow breaths in through your nose and out through your mouth to calm those nerves. Grounding exercises, like focusing on what's around you—the feel of the grass under your feet, the sound of the ball hitting the ground—can also anchor you in the present moment and ease that anxiety.

See Setbacks as Opportunities

Finally, setbacks. Ugh, they can sting, right? But hey, they're not the end of the world. They can be opportunities in disguise. Think of each setback as a lesson. Maybe you missed a goal or made a mistake during practice. Instead of beating yourself up, ask yourself what you can learn from it. How can you improve next time? This shift in perspective turns those setbacks into stepping stones toward becoming a better player.

Fun Fact:

Thierry Henry is Arsenal's all-time leading goal scorer, with 228 goals scored for the club!

Did you know?

Henry has a lifelong fear of frogs, once admitting in an interview that he couldn't stand being anywhere near them!

Using Positive Self-Talk Like a Champ

Recognizing the difference between positive and negative self-talk is important for building confidence. Imagine being on the soccer field, about to take a penalty kick. If your inner voice starts saying stuff like "What if I miss?" or "I'm awful at this," that's negative self-talk creeping in. This kind of mental chatter can shake your confidence and affect your performance negatively.

On the flip side, positive self-talk can sound like, "I've practiced this a hundred times; I've got this" or "Stay calm and focused."

Shifting from negative to positive self-talk isn't just about being blindly optimistic; it's about creating a mental environment where you set yourself up for success rather than failure.

Train Your Brain

The good news is that you can train your brain to lean more toward positive self-talk. It starts with awareness. Pay attention to your thoughts when you're practicing or playing. When you catch yourself thinking negatively, stop and challenge those thoughts. Ask yourself if they're true or if you're just being unnecessarily harsh on yourself. Replace those negative thoughts with more constructive, encouraging ones. It's not about lying to yourself but giving yourself realistic, positive reinforcement. This skill doesn't come overnight, but with consistent effort, you will notice a shift in how you talk to yourself and, consequently, in your confidence levels.

Make Yourself Mantras

Developing personal mantras is another powerful way to reinforce positivity and confidence during challenges. A mantra is a short, powerful phrase that you repeat to yourself to stay motivated and focused. Think of it like your own personal hype song. For instance, if you're feeling nervous before a game, repeating something like "I am strong, I am ready" can help center your mind and boost your confidence. The key is to choose words that resonate with you. Your mantra should make you feel empowered and ready to tackle whatever comes your way.

Creating a personal mantra involves a little introspection. Think about what you need to hear when you're under pressure. If you tend to get anxious, maybe something calming like "Breathe and believe" works best. If you struggle with self-doubt, perhaps "I am capable and prepared" might be more fitting. Write down a few options and try them out during practice or even daily activities. Notice which one makes you feel the most confident, and stick with that. Over time, your mantra can become a reliable tool in your mental toolkit, helping you stay grounded and positive during high-pressure situations.

Be Kind

Another essential aspect of positive self-talk is encouraging athletes to be kind to themselves. We often talk to ourselves in ways we would never talk to a friend. If a teammate misses a goal, you wouldn't berate them and call them names, right? So why do that to yourself? Being kind in your self-talk means treating yourself with the same compassion and understanding that you would offer to others. Positive self-talk doesn't mean ignoring mistakes but rather acknowledging them and then focusing on what you learned and how you can improve.

One technique is to imagine talking to yourself as if you were your own best friend. Instead of "I screwed up, I'm hopeless," you might say, "That didn't go as planned, but I know I can do better next time." This shift may seem small, but it can have a massive impact on your overall confidence. Remember, everyone makes mistakes; it's part of learning and growing. By treating yourself kindly, you create a supportive inner dialogue that builds resilience rather than tearing yourself down.

Focus on the Good

Actively noting successes is another way to build a habit of positivity and motivation. When you're caught up in the chaos of sports and life, it's easy to forget to take note of your achievements, especially the small ones. However, taking the time to acknowledge even minor successes can create a positive mental snowball effect. Maybe you executed a perfect pass in practice, scored a goal in a scrimmage, or simply showed up to training even when you didn't feel like it. Each of these is a success worth noting.

One practical way to track these successes is by keeping a success journal. At the end of each day, jot down a couple of things you did well, no matter how small they might seem. Over time, you'll build a collection of positive experiences that you can look back on, especially when you're feeling down or unsure of yourself. This practice shifts your focus from what didn't go right to what did, reinforcing a positive mindset and bolstering your confidence.

Positive self-talk isn't just a feel-good concept; it has real, measurable effects on performance. Research shows that athletes who engage in positive self-talk perform better in their sports. For example, a study found that students who practiced positive self-talk held their balance longer in a physical test compared to those who engaged in negative self-talk (Wilson, 2019). This suggests that what we tell ourselves directly impacts our physical abilities and outcomes. So, by investing time and effort into developing a routine of positive self-talk, you're giving yourself a competitive edge.

Wrap it Up!

As we wrap up, remember that building self-confidence isn't magic; it's all about consistent effort. Whether it's jotting down affirmations in a journal, picturing yourself nailing that perfect goal, or setting small, manageable challenges, these daily practices can make a huge difference. Listening to feedback is also key—think of it as treasure hunting for ways to improve. Each little step helps you become more confident and capable on the soccer field.

So, whenever you feel a bit shaky, just recall Alex's example and how he turned simple techniques into a confidence-boosting routine. It's not about instant results but rather steady progress. Keep practicing these strategies and watch your self-assurance grow. You'll find that both your game and your mindset will improve, making those soccer challenges less daunting and way more fun.

Handling pressure and stress is something every young athlete deals with, especially on game days. Whether it's those butterflies in the stomach or that little voice in your head saying you're not good enough, anxiety can sneak up on anyone. But guess what? Those feelings are completely normal! Understanding this can make a huge difference in how you approach the game. In the next chapter, we'll be exploring ways to beat those game-day jitters before they get the best of you!

CHAPTER 4

Handling Pressure and Stress

I had to lift the players' expectations. They should never give in. I said that to them all the time: 'If you give in once, you'll give in twice. –Sir Alex Ferguson

Danny stood on the sidelines, watching his teammates run through their warm-up drills. His palms were sweaty, and his heart raced. It was the championship game, and all he could think about was how badly he wanted to impress everyone. "What if I miss a shot? Or worse, what if I let a goal in?" he thought. His mind began to fill with doubt.

"Hey, Danny!" called out Mark, the team captain. "You good? You look a bit pale."

"Yeah, just... nervous, I guess," Danny replied, trying to brush it off.

Mark nodded and came over. "It's fine to feel that way. Remember what we talked about last week? Just focus on your breathing for a second."

Danny took a deep breath, inhaling slowly and holding it for a count of four, just like they practiced. "In...two...three...four," he whispered to himself. Then he held it. "One...two...three...four...five...six...seven." Finally, he exhaled. "It helps, doesn't it?" Mark smiled, knowing that this was a huge moment for Danny.

"Yeah, a little," Danny admitted. "But what about the pressure? Everyone's counting on me."

Mark placed a reassuring hand on Danny's shoulder. "Just remember, we're a team. We win together or lose together. Play your game and have fun. That's what matters."

Handling pressure and stress is a natural part of playing soccer, especially for young athletes gearing up for game day. Whether you're feeling those nervous butterflies or dealing with that little voice doubting your abilities, it's important to know these feelings are normal. Once you understand this, you're already on the right track to managing them better.

In this chapter, we'll dive into some practical techniques to help you manage anxiety and stress so you can focus on performing your best. From creating a consistent pre-game routine and mastering deep-breathing exercises to using visualization techniques and understanding how light physical activities can ease your mind, you'll find helpful strategies tailored just for you. By the end of this chapter, you'll have a toolkit to turn game-day jitters into energy that works for you and helps you enjoy the sport even more.

Managing Game-Day Anxiety

Dealing With the Jitters

First off, let's talk about recognizing pre-game nerves. It's OKAY to feel a bit anxious before a big match. Most athletes do. Instead of seeing it as a bad thing, try looking at it as your body getting ready to perform. Think of it like a superhero getting pumped up for action. The adrenaline rush can give you extra energy and focus. So, next time you feel those jitters, remind yourself that it's just your body gearing up to help you play your best.

Getting Hyped

Now, let's dive into creating a pre-game routine. Having a set routine can be a game-changer (pun intended). It's all about figuring out what works best for you and sticking to it. Maybe you start by listening to your favorite pump-up song, followed by a series of stretches, and end with some positive self-talk. The key here is consistency. When you do the same things before each game, your brain starts to associate those actions with getting ready to perform. This can help lower your anxiety levels because your mind knows what to expect. Make sure to include calming activities in your routine to keep those nerves in check. This could be something like reading a few pages of a book you love or practicing some deep breathing exercises.

Strike a Pose

Speaking of routines, have you ever heard of the "Power Pose"? It's a simple yet effective technique to boost your confidence. A Power Pose is all about using your body language in a way that tricks your brain into feeling more powerful. For instance, stand tall with your hands on your hips like Superman or Wonder Woman for just two minutes. Studies have shown that doing this can lower stress hormones and increase feelings of confidence. Give it a try before your next game. You might feel a bit silly at first, but it can make a difference.

Get Moving

On the topic of being active, engaging in light physical activity before a game can also help ease anxiety. A gentle warm-up can get your blood flowing without tiring you out. Think of a light jog, some jumping jacks, or even dancing around to your favorite tune. The goal here isn't to exhaust yourself but to get rid of that nervous energy. As a bonus, moving your body can release endorphins, which are natural mood boosters.

Combining these strategies can set you up for success. Start with acknowledging that it's okay to feel nervous. Then, develop a solid pre-game routine that includes calming and energizing activities. Don't forget to strike a Power Pose for that extra boost of confidence, and fit in some light physical activity to shake off those jitters.

Give Yourself Grace

One important thing to remember is to be patient with yourself. Anxiety doesn't disappear overnight, but with practice, you'll find what works best for you. Every athlete is different, so don't be afraid to experiment with various techniques until you find your perfect mix. Keep at it, and you'll soon notice that managing pre-game anxiety becomes second nature.

If you can master handling pressure and stress, not only will your performance improve, but you'll also enjoy the game a lot more. After all, soccer is supposed to be fun! So, whether you're playing in a local league or aiming for the pros, these tips can help you stay calm, focused, and ready to give it your all.

Remember, everyone experiences anxiety differently, so what works wonders for one person might not be as effective for another. It's crucial to discover your strategies and stick with them. Over time, you'll build a toolkit that helps you handle any amount of pressure.

Breathing Exercises and Mindfulness Practices

Alright, team, game day is here. You're feeling the butterflies in your stomach, and maybe some of them are turning into annoying little dragons breathing fire. No worries, we've got some tricks up our sleeves to make sure those dragons turn back into butterflies—or, better yet, disappear entirely.

Deep Breathing

First off, let's talk about deep breathing techniques. You might think breathing is something you already know how to do, but trust me, there's an art to it when it comes to managing stress. The goal here is to control your breath to help keep your nerves in check. A good place to start is with the "4-7-8" technique. Inhale quietly through your nose for a count of four, hold your breath for a count of seven, and then exhale completely through your mouth for a count of eight. Not only does this pattern help slow down your heart rate, but it also gives you something else to focus on besides the pressure of the game. Try doing this a few times if you catch yourself feeling overwhelmed.

Mindful Meditation

Okay, now that we've got you breathing like a pro, let's shift gears to mindfulness meditation practices. Mindfulness is all about staying present and not letting your mind wander off into worrying about what could go wrong. Sounds easy, right? Well, it takes a bit of practice. One simple way to get started is by paying attention to your senses for a minute or two. Notice what you see around you, listen to any sounds, and maybe even pay attention to how the grass feels under your cleats. This can anchor you to the present moment and keep you from getting lost in anxious thoughts. Remember, the more you practice, the better you'll get at tuning out distractions and focusing on what's important—playing your best game.

Keep a Journal

Now, let's talk about journaling to express thoughts and feelings. Writing can be a powerful way to process emotions and alleviate stress. You don't need to be Shakespeare to benefit from putting pen to paper. Before a game, try jotting down what's on your mind—your worries, your excitement, and even your game plan. Sometimes, just acknowledging these feelings can take their power away. Plus, having a written record can help you track your progress and notice patterns in your thoughts and emotions over time. Maybe you'll find out that the things you're worried about rarely actually happen, which can be reassuring.

Be Grateful

Another great mindfulness practice is gratitude. Taking a moment to reflect on what you're thankful for can shift your focus from anxiety to appreciation. Before the game, gather with your teammates and have a quick circle. Each person can share something like why they play the game because it's Fun! This reminds everyone to be grateful for the day and just the opportunity to play the game. This exercise can create a positive atmosphere and remind everyone of the bigger picture beyond the competition.

Breath Counting

Breath counting is another mindfulness exercise. All you need to do is sit quietly and count your breaths. Inhale, then exhale and say "one" to yourself. Inhale again, exhale and say "two," and so on. If your mind starts to wander and you lose track, simply go back to "one." This practice is great for centering yourself and can be done just about anywhere, whether in the locker room or even while waiting for the game to start. It's a quick, easy way to regain your focus and calm any racing thoughts.

Do It as a Team

Team rituals can create a feeling of belonging and purpose. These can be as simple as a pre-game chant, a secret handshake, or sharing a unique snack. Whatever it is, these rituals foster connection and help everyone feel more relaxed when they're part of something meaningful. Make sure to settle on a few that resonate with your team and stick to them. This sense of routine can soothe nerves and create excitement.

Feedback Loop

Create a feedback loop for continuous improvement. After each practice or game, spend a few moments discussing not just what went wrong but also what went right. Share feedback with kindness and encouragement. This helps build each other up and fosters an environment of growth and support. It can also reinforce positive behaviors and habits, making everyone feel appreciated and motivated to work harder.

Remind each other that mindfulness can be a journey and that it's perfectly okay to experience a whirlwind of emotions, whether under pressure during practices or games. Encourage one another to practice these techniques regularly, ensuring they become second nature. The more you integrate these mindfulness practices, the more resilient your team will become, transforming those pesky dragons back into butterflies that uplift your spirits as you step onto the field.

Fun Fact:

Ronaldinho won the FIFA World Player of the Year twice and is known for his flashy dribbling, creativity, and incredible free kicks!

Did you know?

Ronaldinho's smile became so famous that he was nicknamed "The Smiling Assassin" because he could destroy defenders with a grin on his face!

How Pro Athletes Handle Pressure

Handling pressure and stress on game day is a critical skill for young soccer players. To illustrate how effective strategies can make a difference, let's look at real-life examples of athletes successfully managing pressure. These stories can inspire young players to adopt similar techniques.

Take the case of Cristiano Ronaldo's iconic game-winning moment in the 2016 UEFA European Championship final. Portugal and France were deadlocked in extra time, and the tension was palpable. Despite an early injury that took him out of the game, Ronaldo stayed on the sidelines, supporting his team with unwavering determination. When Eder scored the winning goal for Portugal, Ronaldo's emotional and mental resilience was evident. He managed his anxiety by channeling it into leadership, showing that even off-field presence can be a powerful tool against pressure.

Now, turning to the younger generation, let's hear some inspiring stories from peers who have conquered pressure in various competitions. Take Emily, a high school soccer forward who struggled with pre-game jitters. She found her breakthrough by developing a routine that included listening to her favorite songs and visualizing her best performances. This simple yet effective strategy helped ground her, reducing her anxiety and allowing her to focus on the game. Her story shows that finding personal rituals can be hugely beneficial.

Then there's Caleb, a goalie who faced immense pressure during penalty shootouts. Being a goalie might be the highest-pressure position ever! He adopted deep-breathing exercises taught by his coach, which helped slow his heart rate and clear his mind. This practice not only improved his performance but also boosted his confidence, demonstrating how breathing techniques can be vital in managing game-time stress.

It's also interesting to compare how athletes manage pressure similarly in life situations outside of sports. For instance, consider how a student preparing for a crucial exam uses tactics similar to those used by athletes. They might break down their study material into smaller and more manageable chunks, take regular breaks between study sessions, and practice mindfulness to help them stay calm. Similarly, athletes prepare for high-pressure moments by breaking down plays, practicing consistently, and using mental exercises to stay focused.

Stories like these from both within and outside the sports world support the importance of mental preparation and resilience. They demonstrate that successful management of pressure isn't just about physical powers but also involves strategic thinking, emotional control, and mental strength.

Wrap it Up!

We've covered a lot of ground in this chapter, from taming those pesky pre-game jitters to embracing the Power Pose like a superhero. By recognizing that nerves are normal and establishing a solid routine filled with confidence-boosting and calming activities, you're setting yourself up for success on the field. Remember, combining deep breathing, light physical activity, and visualization can transform game day from nerve-wracking to empowering. Each technique is a tool in your mental toolkit, helping you stay calm, focused, and ready to give it your all.

The key takeaway here is patience and practice. Everyone deals with anxiety differently, so take your time finding what works best for you. Whether it's listening to your favorite pump-up song or visualizing that perfect goal, these strategies are designed to help you not just perform better but also enjoy the game more. Soccer is meant to be fun, after all! So go out there, experiment with these techniques, and build your personalized approach to managing game-day stress. With practice, handling pressure will soon become second nature, and you'll be able to focus on what truly matters—playing your best and having a blast.

Imagine yourself dribbling down the field, adrenaline pumping through your veins, and suddenly, you spot an opening. The crowd is roaring, but in that instant, you're so focused that everything else fades away. It sounds like magic, but it's all about mastering the art of concentration. In the next chapter, we'll be unlocking the secret to this game-changing skill.

CHAPTER 5

Developing Focus and Concentration

The most important quality a player can have is not skill but mentality. –Jose Mourinho

In a lively little town, there lived a young soccer whiz named Leo. Quick on his feet and full of energy, Leo loved playing soccer, but sometimes his mind would take little vacation breaks during games. (That's a nice way of saying....he's like a squirrel chasing after a new shiny object every 2 minutes!). One day, his coach spotted his talent and decided it was time for a little chat. "Hey Leo, you've got the skills that can light up the field, but we need to tighten up your focus," the coach said with a grin. Leo nodded, scratching his head in confusion but eager to learn. That night, Leo went home and pondered his coach's advice. He wanted to be the best player he could be, but how could he do that if his mind was off daydreaming about snacks and video games?

You know, developing focus and concentration in soccer is just as crucial as mastering that perfect kick. Ever felt like you were trying to juggle a soccer ball, a sandwich, and a basketball at the same time, only to mess it all up? Yep, that can happen on the field too! But here's the cool part: just like you train your legs to sprint faster or your arms to throw harder, you can train your brain to stay super sharp and totally in the zone.

In this chapter, we're swapping out those pesky daydreams for drills that'll keep your brain laser-focused on the game. We're diving deep into why focus is your secret weapon for success in soccer and how it shapes your performance. We'll explore how to keep your mind clear when the pressure's on, juggle those mental tasks like a pro, and ninja your way through distractions. With fun and practical techniques—from routines that ground you before the match to mindfulness exercises that keep your head in the game—you'll be armed with a whole toolkit of strategies to supercharge your concentration and bring your A-game every time. Ready to level up your mental game? Let's kick things off!

The Role of Focus in Performance

Before you even step onto the field, the game already kicks off in your mind. This mental warm-up is key for making quick decisions and executing those sweet moves when it's go-time. Let's get into why keeping your head in the game is so vital and how it can level up your performance.

Stay Focused

Dropping your focus at the wrong moment could mean losing the ball or blowing a golden goal-scoring chance. Focus is your ultimate sidekick! It empowers you to shine even when the heat is on. Let's say it's your turn for a penalty kick. That takes serious concentration! You've got to block out the roar of the crowd, ignore the goalkeeper trying to play mind games, and laser-focus on where you want that ball to go. When you zero in on that one task, your chances of scoring shoot up like a rocket. It's like having tunnel vision, where everything fades away except for your target.

One sunny afternoon, after a hard-hitting practice, a young player named Jake sat down with his coach, slurping on an energy drink. The coach shared an inspiring tale about Michael, a pro soccer player who once battled to keep his focus during matches. Despite his immense talent, Michael's performance plummeted, turning him into a shadow of himself. Frustrated, he sought help and discovered focus techniques that transformed his game. By practicing mindfulness and visualization, Michael eventually led his team to a championship victory! His journey shows just how powerful focus strategies can be.

Choosing Right

Ever felt like your brain was ready to explode during a game? That's what we call cognitive load! Soccer isn't just a test of physical prowess; it's like a mental chess match. Learning about cognitive load helps you make smart choices when the heat is on. The key is knowing how much info your brain can juggle at once so you can sort out your game plan during a match.

Think about when you're charging up the field. You're scanning for open teammates, keeping an eye on the opponent's formation, and deciding whether to pass, shoot, or keep sprinting like a cheetah! If your brain is overloaded, your decision-making can slow down, leading to mistakes. Understanding your mental limits and working within them makes you a pro. Research shows that athletes who manage their cognitive resources crush it on the field (Persaud, 2022).

Let's hear from some champs who faced and conquered huge challenges. Meet Sarah, a young goalkeeper who often felt like she was drowning in a sea of thoughts during nail-biting matches. She worried about letting her team down, recalled coaching tips, and dealt with the weight of the game. This mental chaos affected her game. Determined to rise, Sarah started practicing her selective attention skills, which helped her prioritize key tasks and block out distractions. She learned to mentally compartmentalize, focusing sharply on just the ball and her movements. Thanks to her newfound focus, Sarah helped her team clinch a victory in a tense penalty shootout, proving that overcoming cognitive overload is doable with the right techniques.

Routines

Let's chat routines! Ever notice how some players have quirky little rituals before they take a free kick or penalty? Whether it's bouncing the ball, taking a deep breath, or taking a specific number of steps back, these routines are more than just fun— they're focus-building tools! Establishing pre-game and in-game routines can supercharge your concentration.

Before a match, visualize different game scenarios—this primes your brain for what's ahead, easing anxiety and sharpening focus. During the game, simple habits like breathing exercises can keep you grounded, even when the pressure's cranked up. Find a routine that clicks with you; it can work wonders!

Routines bring structure to the chaotic energy of a soccer match, acting as anchors to keep your mind present. When you stick to a routine, you create a stable mental state, boosting your focus and play.

Dodging Distractions

Distractions are everywhere: an annoying chant from the rival fans, a teammate calling for the ball at the wrong moment, or even self-doubt creeping in. Learning to spot and handle these distractions can skyrocket your in-game focus.

Start by becoming aware of your distractors. Are they external, like noise and visuals, or internal, like negative thoughts? Once you identify what they are, you can develop a plan. For external distractions, selective attention can be your best friend—train your mind to only pick up on relevant cues while zoning out the rest.

Dealing with internal distractions might need a sprinkle of mindfulness. This means acknowledging chaotic thoughts without letting them knock you off your game. Focusing on your breath or looking at a point in the distance can center you, especially during crucial moments.

And let's not forget about game-day jitters! Building mental toughness through practice and simulation drills can help you stay calm and focused when the stakes are high. A clear mind means better decisions and quicker moves!

Now, let's shine a spotlight on everyday heroes—awesome kids like you—who've successfully used these focus strategies. Meet Josh, a 14-year-old midfielder who used to let every little thing break his concentration. From shoelaces coming undone to fans shouting, nothing was off-limits for distractions! One game day, his coach introduced him to easy techniques like deep breathing and setting mini-goals during practice. Josh practiced these tips and saw a massive boost in his focus. Rather than getting flustered by chaos, he learned to channel his attention back to the game. By the end of the season, he was named the most valuable player! Josh's story proves that with focus techniques, everyday kids can become extraordinary players.

A focused mindset isn't just a nice to have; it's a must for excelling on the soccer field. By understanding how focus and performance connect, managing mental load for smarter decisions, creating solid routines to maintain concentration, and handling distractions, you're on your way to being a sharper athlete!

> **Fun Fact:**
>
> Neymar scored 100 goals for three different clubs—Santos, Barcelona, and Paris Saint-Germain—by the age of 29!
>
> *Did you know?*
>
> Neymar loves acting so much that he made a cameo appearance in the TV series "Money Heist" as a monk!

Improving Your Concentration

Boosting your concentration isn't just about sharpening your mind—it's a total game-changer on the field! Here are some super practical exercises and techniques to help elevate your focus skills.

Focus Conditioning Drills

On the field, drills aimed at enhancing concentration can skyrocket your game! Try these during your solo practice sessions. One fun drill involves setting up cones in a cool pattern and dribbling the ball around them while keeping your head up. This helps you concentrate on cone placement and ball control, improving your focus and dribbling skills.

Another fun exercise is the "three-ball juggle." Pair up with a buddy and pass three balls between you as quickly as possible. This chaotic drill demands intense concentration under pressure, sharpening your focus like never before.

You can also try a "shadowing" drill. Team up with a friend and mirror each other's movements. It's a blast and boosts your focus, reaction time, and coordination—all while having fun together!

Conditioning drills aren't just physical training; they're brain workouts, too! Mix up your routine with drills that push quick decision-making and rapid shifts in focus, keeping training exciting and your mind sharp.

Time Management in Personal Training

Time management isn't just about following a schedule; it's about maximizing every moment of your training. The best athletes dedicate time to honing their skills outside team practices. By assigning specific times to different training components, you can give each part the focus it deserves!

For example, start with 15 minutes of warm-up drills, then dive into 20 minutes of skill training, and wrap up with 15 minutes of cool-down exercises. Breaking your sessions into chunks helps you concentrate fully on each part. Use a timer to keep track of your segments, and challenge yourself to stay focused until it goes off!

Reflection is key, too. After each practice, take a moment to jot down what went well and what you can work on. Write your observations and set goals for your next session. This not only sharpens your focus during training but also helps track your progress and continuously improve.

Improving your concentration takes time and effort, but the results are worth it! Whether you practice mindfulness to stay present, use visualization for mental prep, engage in focus drills, or manage your training time effectively, each method builds your skills as an athlete.

Staying Present on Game Day

Being fully engaged during soccer games is essential for young athletes aiming to step up their performance and decision-making skills. It's not just about kicking skills; mental focus plays a huge role in how well you play. Let's explore techniques that help you stay rooted in the present, amp up your composure, manage your emotions, and strengthen team dynamics.

Techniques for Staying Present

One of the first steps to sharpening your focus is learning how to stay present. This means ditching thoughts of past oopsies or future worries and honing in on what's happening right now. Mindfulness is a fantastic method for this.

Mindfulness is about practicing attention and awareness. Set aside 5-20 minutes daily to zero in on something simple—like breathing, a sound, or even shining your cleats. When your mind drifts, gently guide it back. With practice, you'll train your brain to stay focused during games.

You can also engage in casual mindfulness during everyday tasks. When riding your bike, concentrate on the feel of your pedal strokes. When distractions come up—like dinner plans—bring your attention back to the pedals. This gentle redirection helps you stay present and eases game pressure (Henriksen, 2022).

The Power of Breath

Breathing techniques are super powerful for maintaining composure and focus on the field. When anxiety or overwhelm arise, breathing can center you back to the game.

Deep breathing is a simple technique where you inhale slowly through your nose, filling your lungs. Hold it for a couple of seconds, and then exhale through your mouth. This calms your heart rate and calms your nerves. You can use this trick anytime, whether on a break in the game or before a penalty kick!

Box breathing is another essential technique. Inhale for four counts, hold for four, exhale for four, and hold again for four. This rhythmic pattern helps you regain control and focus if your concentration starts to slip.

Emotional Awareness

Being aware of your emotions is crucial for maintaining presence and focus. Recognizing how your feelings affect your performance can greatly enhance your concentration.

When you notice your emotions, you can take steps to manage them. If you feel frustrated after missing a shot, acknowledge that feeling, but don't let it overwhelm you. Instead, use it as a signal to recalibrate and think about your next move. One way to improve emotional awareness is through journaling. Write down how you felt during practice or a game and how it impacted your performance. Over time, you'll spot patterns and learn to handle different emotions better.

Gelling with Your Team

Connecting with your teammates can boost focus all around. Soccer is a team sport, and when everyone is mentally present, the whole squad benefits. Open communication strengthens your unity. Knowing your teammates' strengths and weaknesses makes it easier to make quick decisions and execute plays.

Team-building activities, like passing drills with name-calling, can enhance both communication and focus. During the game, small gestures—like eye contact or a thumbs-up—show support and keep everyone locked in!

Setting up pre-game rituals together can deepen your connection as a team. Whether it's a team cheer, a specific warm-up routine, or a quick huddle, these ritualistic practices create shared focus and a mental switch for total game-mode concentration.

Remember, every player has moments when they drift or feel stressed. What sets successful athletes apart is their ability to recognize those instances and refocus on what matters. By honing your ability to stay present, use your breath, manage emotions, and connect with your team, you'll elevate not only your own game but also your team's performance.

Wrap it Up!

Focus is like your very own soccer superpower! In this chapter, we've tackled the importance of keeping your eyes on the ball (literally and metaphorically). From cruising down the field without tripping over your own feet to nailing that pressure-filled penalty kick, staying focused can flip the script. We also discussed how dealing with cognitive overload is like juggling flaming soccer balls—you've got to keep your cool, or it's game over. Knowing your brain's limits helps you play smart and hard!

We've dropped handy routines and tips to keep distractions at bay, whether they're rowdy fans or pesky doubts. Anchors like pre-game rituals, mindful breathing, and visualization can dial your game up from "meh" to "wow!" Think of these techniques as your secret weapons, ready to roll when the going gets tough. By mastering focus, you'll not only sharpen your skills but also rack up those "Player of the Match" titles faster than you can shout "goal!" Keep practicing, keep focusing, and soon you'll realize just how game-changing it truly is.

Building resilience is like trying to dribble a soccer ball through a maze of chicken coops—challenging, unpredictable, and a little messy! Just like you learn to navigate coops (or dodge chickens), you can bounce back from setbacks and keep your head in the game. We'll uncover more about resilience in the next chapter.

CHAPTER 6

Resilience and Overcoming Setbacks

I always believed in pushing myself to be my best and that hard work and determination would pay off. I learned that success in football is not just about talent but also about putting in the effort to improve every day. –Thierry Henry

Liam stared at the ground, his heart heavy after the game. The final whistle had barely echoed before he felt the sting of defeat wrap around him like a heavy blanket. They had lost the championship match, and despite giving it his all, it didn't seem enough. "I missed that last penalty," he mumbled to himself, his voice just a whisper amid the chatter of his teammates. "If only I had practiced more." His friend Jason approached, concern flickering in his eyes. "Hey, it was a tough game, but we played as a team. You're not alone in this," he said, nudging Liam gently.

In this chapter, you'll discover why it's normal to feel bummed out after a loss and how to handle those emotions without bottling them up like a fizzy drink ready to explode. You'll also get some tips on how to look at failures not as the end of the world but as golden opportunities to up your game. Plus, we'll chat about building a solid support squad—think coaches, teammates, and maybe even your parents yelling encouragement from the sidelines. By the end, you'll have a playbook full of strategies to help you face challenges head-on and come out kicking stronger than ever.

Coping With Losses and Failures

Building resilience in players requires more than just physical training and skill development. It's essential to equip them with strategies to effectively cope with losses and failures, as these experiences are part of any athlete's journey. This section explores critical ways to help young athletes handle setbacks and emerge stronger.

Understanding Emotional Responses

One of the first steps to developing resilience is understanding emotional responses. It's normal for young athletes to feel disappointed after a loss or failure. These feelings are natural and necessary for recovery. Instead of stamping on them, athletes should recognize and accept them. Acknowledging disappointment helps athletes process their disappointment and move on to focus on what they want to achieve next.

Reframing Failure

After acknowledging emotions, the next step is to reframe failure. Instead of seeing a loss as the end of the world, athletes can view it as an opportunity for growth. Focusing on what can be learned from each setback rather than dwelling on the defeat encourages a positive mindset. For example, if a player missed a crucial goal during a game, instead of fixating on the miss, they could analyze why it happened. Was it a lack of focus? Poor technique? By identifying the cause, they can work on improving that specific area in future training sessions. There's no world in which telling yourself "I suck!" helps!

Think about some of the greatest soccer players. They didn't become successful by only winning; their progress often came from learning through their mistakes. Every error and every loss brought valuable insights that contributed to their growth. Reframing failures doesn't make losses less painful, but it gives them purpose and turns them into stepping stones for future success.

Building Your Squad

After a disappointing game, talking to a coach can provide new perspectives and constructive feedback. Teammates who are going through similar experiences can offer encouragement and camaraderie, making the tough times more manageable. Establishing a solid support system means knowing there's always someone to lean on, which is incredibly empowering.

Creating a Recovery Plan

Developing a practical recovery plan is essential for bouncing back after a loss. This plan should include specific training focuses and minor goals aimed at addressing weaknesses highlighted by the setback. For example, if a young player struggles with endurance in a match, their recovery plan might include conditioning exercises to improve stamina.

A recovery plan is like a road map back to confidence and peak performance. It breaks down the daunting task of "getting better" into manageable steps, each small goal achieved acting as a milestone. These minor successes are vital—they build momentum and restore self-belief. Additionally, having a structured plan provides a sense of control and direction, reducing the anxiety that can come with feeling lost after a defeat.

Practical Ways to Building Resilience

Alright, it's time to roll up our sleeves and get practical. Building resilience isn't just about toughing it out; there are actual techniques you can use. Let's break it down:

Pick Your Battles

Set goals that address your specific adversities. If you struggle with stamina, set a goal to improve your endurance through specific drills and running exercises. By focusing on your weaknesses, you can turn them into strengths.

Picture It

Picture yourself in challenging situations and think about how you'd handle them. Visualization is key here. Imagine yourself scoring that penalty you once missed or recovering quickly if you make a mistake. This practice helps you stay focused and ready when the real deal happens.

Put It to the Test

Sometimes, stepping out of your comfort zone in different areas can help build resilience. Try a fun activity like rock climbing or martial arts. Nothing serious that takes up too much time (because, hey, you're a soccer player!) But these sports demand mental toughness and can translate over to your soccer performance.

Celebrating Small Wins

In the journey of overcoming setbacks, it's crucial to recognize and celebrate progress, no matter how minor it may seem. Did you manage to run a bit faster today? Celebrate! Did you juggle the ball five times without dropping it? High five!

Celebrating these small victories helps maintain a positive outlook. It encourages you to keep pushing forward, even when the going gets tough. Remember, every little win is a step toward your bigger goals. By acknowledging your progress, you boost your morale and reinforce the belief that you can overcome future hurdles.

Inspirational Comeback Stories

Soccer history is filled with stories of players who have overcome significant challenges and made remarkable comebacks. An inspiring tale is that of Cristiano Ronaldo. Do you remember earlier, we talked about how he grew up on a tiny island? Ronaldo faced numerous challenges growing up. His family didn't have much money, and he wasn't near any cities with big soccer associations. Despite these hardships, his passion and dedication to soccer never wavered. At just 12, he moved hundreds of miles away from home to join Sporting Lisbon's academy. Through sheer willpower and relentless training, Ronaldo transformed himself into one of the best players in the world, winning multiple Ballon d'Or awards. His story exemplifies how resilience can lead to extraordinary success.

Encouraging young athletes to share their own comeback stories can be incredibly motivational and foster stronger bonds within teams. Everyone has faced setbacks, whether it's recovering from an injury, dealing with personal issues, or overcoming performance slumps. Sharing these experiences reminds athletes that they are not alone in their struggles and can inspire their peers to keep pushing forward.

The Power of People

A supportive community can play a crucial role in helping athletes overcome setbacks.

Remember that story about David Beckham facing tough times? When he got that red card in the 1998 World Cup against Argentina, the media was all over him, and people thought that was the end of his career. But he didn't let it break him. He trained harder and came back stronger, becoming one of the best free-kick takers ever. It's all about what you do next.

Every great soccer player has faced adversity. They all had moments where they questioned their skills. Ronaldinho, Neymar—look at their ups and downs. They faced injuries and criticism, yet each bounce back was fueled by determination.

Imagine if we could create an atmosphere where everyone feels empowered to learn from their mistakes without fear of judgment, just like how Didier Drogba led Chelsea through tough times. He lost critical matches, too, but he gathered his teammates, motivating them constantly. We can create a culture where losing isn't seen as a failure but as a stepping stone, like how Andrea Pirlo never gave up through setbacks. In 2005, during the UEFA Champions League final, he missed a penalty kick and felt responsible for the team losing! Even though he talks about that moment being the worst of his entire career, Andrea eventually led Italy to victory in the 2006 World Cup. That sounds like a pretty good trade!

Remember, every setback is a chance to learn.

Fun Fact:

Mia Hamm scored 158 international goals, which was the record for most international goals scored by any player, male or female, for nearly two decades!

Did you know?

Mia Hamm was so fast and agile as a child that she played on the boys' soccer team until she was 14 because there weren't any competitive girls' teams in her area!

Maintaining Mental Toughness

Maintaining mental toughness during setbacks can feel like trying to juggle soccer balls in a hurricane, but fear not—strategies exist to keep your head in the game. Let's explore some proven methods that can help young soccer athletes stay mentally strong even when the going gets tough.

Be Mindful

First off, mindfulness practices are like the secret sauce for staying chill under pressure. Think of this as your "mental stretching." Techniques such as meditation and deep breathing exercises are golden for managing stress and keeping your focus sharp. When you're on the field or even during those tough training sessions, taking a moment to concentrate on your breathing can ground you. Meditation isn't just about sitting quietly; it's about bringing your mind back from wandering off into worryland. Even a few minutes a day can make a big difference.

Be Kind to Yourself

Positive self-talk is another powerful tool in your resilience toolkit. Imagine having a personal cheerleader inside your head, always ready with a pep talk when the chips are down. Using affirmations and positive reinforcement can help you build up your confidence and resilience. It's all about taking those negative thoughts and turning them around. Instead of thinking, *I messed up that shot, I'm terrible.* Try telling yourself, *I missed this time, but I'll nail it next time.* It's not about ignoring mistakes but learning to frame them constructively.

Positive self-talk works wonders, especially when things aren't going your way. Picture yourself in the middle of a game where nothing seems to be working. Your passes go astray, and your shots miss the mark. Instead of letting frustration take over, remind yourself of times you excelled. Simple phrases like "I've got this" or "One step at a time" can drastically change your mindset. Think about famous players who use this technique; they constantly reinforce their belief in themselves, which powers them through tough moments.

Be Realistic With Your Goals

Setting realistic goals is essential for maintaining a sense of direction and accomplishment. Break your soccer ambitions into smaller, achievable milestones. Instead of aiming to become the best player overnight, set incremental goals like improving your stamina by running an extra lap each week or perfecting a specific skill. Achievable goals keep your motivation high and offer a sense of progress, which is crucial during setbacks.

Setting realistic goals might seem like common advice, but its impact is profound. If you aim too high too quickly, setbacks can be discouraging. Instead, set smaller, manageable targets that act as stepping stones toward your ultimate goal. For example, if you want to improve your footwork, start with mastering basic drills before advancing to more complex maneuvers. Celebrate each milestone you hit; this keeps you motivated and focused on continual improvement.

To put this into perspective, let's consider Alex, a young soccer athlete who dreams of playing professionally. Alex applies mindfulness by dedicating 10 minutes each day to working on his focus by visualizing himself performing a skill well. It's been helping him remain calm during matches. When faced with criticism or mistakes, Alex uses positive self-talk, reminding himself of his strengths and past successes. He often visualizes scoring key goals and executing flawless plays, boosting his mental preparation. Lastly, Alex sets realistic goals like increasing his weekly training hours gradually and mastering one new skill each month. These strategies collectively build his mental toughness, enabling him to bounce back quickly from any setback he encounters.

Wrap it Up!

Alright, so we've learned the importance of dealing with loss and setbacks like seasoned pros. From understanding those pesky emotions to giving failure a solid reframing, we're loading up our resilience toolkit. Imagine yourself as a young soccer player equipped with strategies to tackle those tough moments. We've talked about leaning on your squad (coaches, teammates, even family) when things get rough and nailing down a recovery plan to bounce back stronger than ever.

Now, picture all these lessons as your secret sauce for becoming not just a better athlete but a more resilient one. Think about how Messi and Ronaldo didn't let their challenges keep them down and how you can channel that same energy. Next time life throws a curveball, you'll be ready to catch it, give it a little spin, and kick it right into the goal. Remember, it's not just about winning every game; it's about learning, growing, and celebrating every small win along the way. So go ahead, face those setbacks head-on, and show the world what you've got!

Teamwork and communication are the unsung heroes of soccer. Sure, you might think it's all about those jaw-dropping goals or that slick dribbling move you've been practicing. But without solid teamwork and top-notch communication, your team's going to look like a bunch of lost tourists trying to find their way around a new city. In the next chapter, we'll be looking at ways you can use teamwork and communication to really up your game!

CHAPTER 7

Teamwork and Communication

I've never scored a goal without getting a pass from someone on my team first. –Abby Wambach

Meet Jamie, a budding soccer superstar who couldn't get enough of the jaw-dropping plays he saw on TV. He was quick and had a pretty solid shot, but when it came to making a real splash on the field, he felt like a fish out of water. During the big moments, the game just seemed to slip through his fingers. One fateful practice, while chilling on the sidelines, Jamie overheard his coach chatting about the magic of teamwork and communication. It sparked an idea! Jamie realized he needed to connect more with his teammates and express himself during games.

That week, he made it his mission to stay after practice and brainstorm strategies with his pals. He'd ask questions like, "How do you prefer to get a pass?" or "What's our best formation?" As practices rolled on, Jamie began to feel the energy shift. He and his best buddy, Alex, even created secret signals to communicate their moves during scrimmages. A quick thumbs-up meant they were ready to execute a sweet corner play, while a tap on his thigh signaled a breakaway pass was on the way. The more they practiced these signals, the more confident Jamie felt, and soon, he was setting up plays and creating chances for others instead of trying to go solo.

In one electrifying game, he and Alex pulled off a perfectly timed play that ended with a cheering crowd going wild after a goal! Talk about an adrenaline rush!

In this chapter, we're diving into how clear communication, nonverbal cues, feedback, and conflict resolution can transform your team from a group of buddies into a powerhouse ready to take on any challenge! You'll learn why shouting "Left!" can lead to chaos and how a simple point can sometimes deliver a stronger message than a thousand words. Feedback isn't just for your report card—it's crucial for leveling up your game! Let's face it: bickering over a bad pass can ruin your vibe faster than slipping on a banana peel during a match. By the end of this chapter, you'll understand how mastering these skills can make your team tighter than a brand-new pair of cleats!

Importance of Straight Talk

Effective communication is the secret sauce for seamless teamwork in soccer. Whether you're practicing on your local pitch or competing in a high-stakes match, how you convey info can make or break your team's performance. Understanding the power of concise messaging, nonverbal signals, feedback, and conflict resolution can seriously elevate your game and your contribution to the team.

Concise Messaging

In soccer, clear and timely communication is a game-changer. Picture yourself zipping down the field, ready to receive a pass. If a teammate yells, "Left!" without clarity, you might wonder—wait, is that their left, my left, or the entire left side of the field? Total confusion! This can lead to missed chances and frustrated teammates.

Concise messaging is all about using clear and specific language everyone understands. Instead of vague commands, stick to universally recognized phrases you agreed upon during practice.

So, instead of shouting "pass," go with "cross" for a side pass, or say "man on!" to alert a teammate about an opponent sneaking up behind them. This clarity makes the game flow smoother and your teamwork stronger!

Guidelines for Concise Messaging

- Use short and specific terms: Ditch the jargon and keep it simple.
- Agree on common phrases: Make sure everyone's on the same page about terms like "switch," "mark," or "drop."
- Project confidence: Clear and assertive instructions pack a punch!

Nonverbal Communication

Words are important, but they're not the whole story on the field. Nonverbal communication—like gestures, facial expressions, and body language—plays a huge role in letting your teammates know what's up.

Imagine a defender tightly marking an attacker. A simple point towards where they should be positioned sends a clear message without saying a word! As a midfielder, a glance at a forward can communicate your intent way better than shouting across the field.

Nonverbal communication is especially handy when the crowd is roaring, drowning out spoken instructions. Plus, it adds an element of surprise against rivals who might catch wind of your plans.

- Create clear signals: Develop a list of hand gestures understood by all players.
- Practice regularly: Ask your coach to help integrate these into your training sessions until they become second nature.
- Mind your body language: Your position and posture send important cues to teammates.

Fun Fact:

Birgit Prinz is a three-time FIFA World Player of the Year (2003, 2004, 2005) and was one of the most dominant strikers in women's football history, leading Germany to back-to-back World Cup titles in 2003 and 2007!!

Did you know?

Birgit Prinz was known to have a dry sense of humor and once joked during an interview that if she wasn't a soccer player, she would have been a carpenter—because at least wood doesn't talk back when you miss a goal!

Feedback

Feedback is all about growth—both for you and the team! Constructive feedback helps everyone understand their strengths and what to work on.

Let's say after a match, your coach holds a team huddle to discuss what went right and where to improve. Instead of just pointing out mistakes, your coach says something like, "Next time, spread out wider on the wing to create more space." This type of actionable feedback helps players adapt and sharpen their skills.

You can take this same approach with your teammates—sharing feedback should be a two-way street that fosters a culture of continuous improvement!

Guidelines for Effective Feedback

- Be specific: Focus on actions, not personal traits.
- Offer improvement suggestions: Highlight areas for growth along with practical solutions.
- Encourage self-assessment: Help each other reflect on performance and identify ways to improve.

Conflict Resolution

Even the best teams occasionally have disagreements. How those conflicts are handled can greatly influence team morale and performance. Picture two players arguing over a misplayed pass during a critical moment. These "beefs" can pull focus from the game and hurt team spirit.

Effective conflict resolution starts with active listening. Make sure everyone has a chance to talk. Sometimes, just feeling heard can ease the tension! Shift the focus from finger-pointing to problem-solving. For example, if you and a teammate disagree on positioning, ask your coach for ideas to try during practice.

Guidelines for Conflict Resolution

- Listen up: Let the other person speak without interruptions.
- Keep your cool: Manage your emotions to avoid making things worse.
- Focus on solutions: Work toward something that everyone can agree on.

Fostering Strong Team Dynamics

Think of the legends in soccer history: their greatness often comes from collaboration and synergy. Each player must blend their unique talents to create a strong unit united in purpose.

Building Trust

Trust is the backbone of any successful team. Without it, even the most talented players struggle to shine. If you hesitate to pass to a teammate because you doubt their abilities, your team's chances can go down the drain. Building trust takes time and consistent effort.

Encourage open discussions about your strengths and weaknesses. Knowing each other's capabilities builds reliability and confidence on the field.

Trust takes time to build, but here are some helpful practices:

- **Open Dialogue:** Is your team a place where you can have honest communication? Or are teammates scared they'll be made fun of or yelled at?
- **Trust-Building Activities:** Talk to your coach about fun exercises, like buddy obstacle courses where one player guides another using verbal cues—great for building trust and communication!
- **Celebrate Success:** Take a moment to recognize and celebrate achievements, no matter how small! Acknowledging wins boosts team spirit and trust.

Fun Fact:

Miroslav Klose holds the record for the most goals scored in FIFA World Cup history, with 16 goals across four tournaments!

Did you know?

Klose was famous for his post-goal celebration, where he would perform an acrobatic front flip—but he stopped doing it later in his career to avoid injuries!

Distinct Roles

A standout soccer team is made up of players with different strengths. That skill diversity helps the team to adapt and enhances overall performance. Trust your teammates to play their role just as you want them to trust you to play yours.

Think of your team like a symphony: each musician plays a different instrument, but when they play together, that's where the magic happens!

Unified Goals and Vision

When each player shares the team's objectives, it creates harmony and friendship. Imagine a ship where all the crew row in sync—smooth sailing! In the same way, players should share a vision and understand how their roles contribute to the team's goals.

Keeping shared objectives alive is an ongoing adventure that requires regular check-ins!

Team Huddles

Invite your teammates to gather after practice for huddles to review goals and highlight how everyone contributes. Each player needs to see their role in achieving success. Regular discussions serve as a platform for open communication and keep progress in check.

Encourage teammates to express thoughts about matches or anything affecting team performance. Involve your coach to provide constructive feedback and facilitate discussion.

Engage in Team-Building Events

Team-building activities are the glue that strengthens connections and boosts communication, leading to better coordination during games. You don't just need to see each other on the pitch; organizing time for some off-the-field fun can help build those bonds. Activities like trust exercises or casual hangouts cultivate unity and camaraderie. A cohesive team thrives both on and off the field!

Chat with your coach about regularly rolling out team-building activities to keep those bonds tight and your atmosphere positive.

Advantages of Strong Teamwork and Communication

Improved teamwork and communication not only elevate individual performance but also enrich team spirit and community vibes. When players unite harmoniously, a supportive environment springs into action! This positive energy extends beyond the field, building community ties and motivating families and fans to rally behind the team.

A fantastic example of this is how grassroots soccer programs focus on teamwork and communication, nurturing talented players, and a strong community spirit. Through soccer, young athletes learn valuable life skills like self-discipline and leadership while forming friendships and confidence that last well beyond the pitch.

Wrap it Up!

In a nutshell, we've explored how to turbocharge teamwork and communication. From concise messaging to nonverbal cues and from constructive feedback to resolving conflicts—these strategies are vital. Think of these skills as building blocks; while they may not shine as brightly as a winning goal, they're what turns a group of individuals into a formidable squad. Your performance is about more than just personal glory; it's about uplifting those around you.

Next time you hit the field, focus on clear communication. Embrace those signals, provide and accept feedback openly, and tackle conflicts calmly. Applying these principles consistently will elevate your team from a collection of players into a powerful force. Enjoy the game, and keep your spirits high!

Visualize stepping onto the field, mentally rehearsing each move while feeling grounded in your thoughts. In the next chapter, we'll discover the magic of imagination and how it can boost your performance—just like some of the greatest athletes out there!

CHAPTER 8

Visualization and Mental Imagery

Every single day, I wake up and commit to myself to become a better player. –Mia Hamm

Famous soccer players like Ronaldinho and Beckham are known for stunning free kicks Apart from hard work and incredible talent, do you know their secret weapon? Visualization. Before every match, they sit quietly, close their eyes, and imagine themselves on the field. Beckham actually sees the ball at his feet, feels the slight breeze, and hears the roaring of the crowd. In his mind, he watches as he successfully curves the ball into the top corner of the net. This practice helps him manage performance anxiety and increases his confidence. By the time he steps onto the actual pitch, he's already "scored" that goal multiple times in his head, making it feel more achievable during the game.

So, what exactly are we diving into here? We'll explore how visualization serves as a mental rehearsal, helping you refine techniques without the sweat. We'll also talk about how picturing successful performances can boost your confidence to new heights. And let's not forget to stay focused; using visualization can help you block out distractions and zero in on your goals. We'll get into how imagining pressurized scenarios can make you more comfortable when they happen. Plus, we'll discuss why engaging all your senses can make these mental drills far more effective. Get ready to take your game from good to great just by using the most powerful tool you have—your mind!

Benefits of Visualization

Visualization and mental imagery can be game-changers in the world of sports, especially for young soccer athletes looking to step up their performance. This part of the chapter will take you through how visualization can significantly enhance athletic performance and mental preparedness.

Preparation

First off, let's talk about how visualization acts as a mental rehearsal. Imagine yourself out on the field, but instead of physically dribbling or shooting, you're doing it all in your mind. You go over every move, every shot, and every strategy. This mental rehearsal helps you refine techniques before actually hitting the field. Think of it as practice without the sweat. You can mentally recreate specific actions and scenarios, which will better prepare your brain and body to perform better when it's game time.

Confidence

Another cool benefit is the boost in confidence that comes from visualization. Athletes often report feeling more assured after they visualize successful performances. When you repeatedly see yourself scoring goals or making perfect passes in your mind, you start to believe that you can do it in real life, too. It's like giving yourself a pep talk but in picture form.

Concentration

Speaking of staying focused, visualization also helps athletes maintain concentration on their goals and strategies by blocking out distractions. Whether it's a big game or just another practice, visualizing your objectives keeps your mind sharp and concentrated. Instead of worrying about the crowd or any external pressures, you're laser-focused on what you need to do to succeed.

Less Pressure

Now, let's tackle how visualization reduces the mental burden of pressure situations. Imagine being in a high-stakes match and feeling the pressure mounting. Visualization allows you to mentally prepare for these moments. By practicing these pressurized scenarios in your head, you become more comfortable handling them in reality. This mental preparation reinforces positive self-beliefs, making you feel more ready and resilient when facing actual challenges.

Visualization isn't just about seeing yourself play; it's about creating a full sensory experience in your mind. Envision the feel of the grass under your cleats, the sound of the whistle, and even the smell of the fresh-cut field. Engaging all your senses can make the mental rehearsal much more effective.

Fun Fact:

Manuel Neuer revolutionized the goalkeeper position with his "sweeper-keeper" style, often coming far out of his penalty area to intercept the ball and act like an extra defender!

Did you know?

Neuer once dressed up as a giant fuzzy bear mascot to prank his Bayern Munich teammates, and none of them knew it was him until he took off the head!

How Does It Help You?

Let's get deeper into how each aspect of visualization can benefit you:

Improving Your Skills

When you visualize, you're essentially training your brain to send signals to your muscles, just as if you were physically acting. For instance, visualizing the exact way you want to kick the ball can help you execute that move more flawlessly in reality. Studies have shown that the brain doesn't differentiate much between an imagined action and a real one, meaning that mental practice can contribute significantly to improved physical performance (Adams, 2009).

Building Confidence

Confidence isn't just born out of hard work; it can also come from the mind. By visualizing successful outcomes, you create a mental record of achievements. Over time, these positive images can pile up, building your confidence layer by layer. When you're confident, you're more likely to take risks, push boundaries, and perform at your best. So, the next time you're nervous before a game, spend some time visualizing your best plays—you'll walk onto the field with a whole new level of assurance.

Blocking Out Distractions

Distractions are everywhere, from the noise of the crowd to the importance of the match. Visualization helps block these out by keeping your focus razor-sharp on your goals and strategy. When you train your mind to concentrate on the task at hand, you're less likely to get sidetracked by external factors. This kind of mental discipline is crucial, especially in tense game situations where one moment of lost focus can cost you the game.

Reducing Pressure

Pressure can either make or break a performance. Visualization helps you cope with it better by preparing you for high-pressure situations. By repeatedly imagining yourself in these intense scenarios, you become more familiar with the feelings and challenges you'll face. This familiarity reduces the mental strain and helps you stay calm and collected, even when the stakes are high.

Staying on Track Despite Setbacks

Injuries are an unfortunate reality for many athletes, but visualization can play a critical role in recovery as well. Take the story of a professional soccer player who suffered a serious knee injury. While sidelined from physical training, he used visualization to maintain mental engagement with the sport. Every day, he imagined himself running drills, feeling the ball at his feet, and making precise passes. This mental practice not only helped keep his skills sharp but also provided emotional healing by keeping his spirits high. By the time he was physically ready to return, he found that his mental preparation had significantly reduced the time needed to regain his form.

Improves Teamwork

When a team practices collective mental preparation strategies, they improve not only individual skills but also communication and anticipation on the field. For instance, a team might visualize key plays together, imagining how they'll move in unison when executing a strategy. This shared mental rehearsal can develop a deeper understanding of each player's role and foster better coordination during real matches. Imagine knowing exactly where your teammate will be positioned, almost telepathically, just because you've both seen the play unfold in your minds countless times before.

Practical Tips for Using Visualization

So, how can you start incorporating visualization into your routine? It's pretty simple and doesn't require any special equipment—just your imagination!

1. First, find a quiet place where you won't be disturbed.
2. Close your eyes and start picturing the game. See yourself performing the actions, not just passively watching them like a movie.
3. Feel the emotions you'd feel during the game—the excitement, the determination, and even the pressure.
4. Imagine executing your skills with perfection, whether it's a precise pass, a powerful shot, or a strategic move.
5. Make these scenarios as vivid and detailed as possible.

The great thing about visualization is that it can be done anytime, anywhere. Whether you're lying in bed before sleep, sitting on the bus, or even brushing your teeth, there's always an opportunity to sneak in a quick visualization session. The more you practice, the more natural it becomes.

Incorporate this technique into your regular training sessions just like you dedicate time to drills and exercises and set aside a few minutes each day for mental rehearsals. Consistent practice will help reinforce neural pathways in the brain, making it easier to translate these mental practices into physical action.

Step-By-Step Guide to Effective Visualization

Create the Right Environment

When it comes to using visualization techniques in soccer training, the first crucial step is creating a peaceful environment. Imagine trying to visualize yourself scoring the winning goal while your little brother bangs on drums in the next room—pretty tough, right? So, find a quiet space where you can focus without distractions. Turn off your phone, close the door, and maybe even ask your family for some quiet time.

Set Your Intentions

Next, let's talk about defining clear intentions. You might be thinking, "What does that even mean?" Simply put, know what you want to achieve before you start visualizing. Whether it's nailing that perfect corner kick or improving your speed during breakaways, having a specific goal will guide your mind during the imagery process. Just like how your coach sets specific drills during practice, setting clear intentions will make your mental practice more effective.

Use All Your Senses

Now, let's spice things up by involving multiple senses during your visualization. Don't just see yourself on the field; feel the grass under your cleats, hear the crowd cheering, smell the crisp air, and even taste the electrolytes at halftime. The more senses you involve, the more real it becomes, which makes your brain think you're experiencing it. This multisensory approach helps bridge the gap between imagination and reality, making your practice sessions far more impactful.

Be Consistent

Consistency is another key element here. Trust me, you wouldn't expect to get better at penalty kicks by practicing once a month, right? Visualization works the same way. Set aside regular time for these sessions, making them part of your daily routine. Maybe spend 10 minutes every evening visualizing your game plan for the next day. And hey, why not keep a journal to track your progress? Write down what you visualized, how you felt, and any improvements you noticed in your actual games. Documenting your experiences not only helps you track progress but also motivates you to stick with it.

Fun Fact:

Philipp Lahm captained Germany to victory in the 2014 FIFA World Cup and is regarded as one of the best full-backs in football history, despite standing at only 5'7"!

Did you know?

Lahm was known for being so clean-cut and well-mannered that he never received a red card throughout his entire professional career!

Increased Focus and Goal Achievement

Alright, let's dive into how visualization can supercharge your performance on the soccer field. The goal here is to explain how picturing your successes not only enhances your focus but also aligns your subconscious with your performance goals.

Game-Plan

Visualization is like a mental game plan. By envisioning desired outcomes, athletes can block out distractions more effectively and maintain their concentration. Imagine yourself stepping onto the field, feeling confident and ready. Visualizing these moments helps you focus entirely on your performance, pushing aside any worries or external disruptions. It's like having a laser-focused mind that's solely zeroed in on winning.

Mental Resilience

Beyond just enhancing focus, visualization fosters a deeper understanding of game scenarios and responses. Picture a tricky situation on the field: Maybe you're facing a tougher opponent, or conditions aren't in your favor. Your ability to mentally rehearse various responses builds mental resilience for these unexpected challenges. It's like simulating your head, so when the real moment comes, you're already prepared. This mental rehearsal reduces anxiety and increases your readiness to tackle anything thrown your way.

Manifesting Success

Another big win with visualization is how it aligns your subconscious with your performance goals. When you consistently visualize success, your brain starts to believe in it. It cultivates a sense of purpose and direction not only during training but also in competition. Think of it as setting your internal GPS toward victory. This alignment means every part of your mind and body is geared toward achieving your goals, making sure you stay motivated and on track.

Motivation

Visualizing both short-term and long-term achievements keeps that motivation engine running smoothly. Short-term goals could be nailing a new technique in practice, while long-term goals might be reaching a championship. By vividly picturing yourself achieving these milestones, you create a powerful connection between the effort you put in and the successful outcomes you desire. For instance, imagine scoring the winning goal in a crucial match. Feel the exhilaration, hear the crowd cheering, and see your teammates celebrating with you. This vivid mental imagery strengthens your resolve and keeps you pushing forward, even on tough days.

It's worth mentioning that visualization isn't just another trendy idea. Famous athletes across the globe swear by it. They've proven time and again that mental rehearsal isn't wishful thinking; it's a deliberate practice that affects your brain in profound ways. When you visualize an action, your brain fires signals as if you were performing it. This kind of mental exercise improves coordination, builds confidence, and ultimately makes success more accessible.

Remember, visualization isn't a magic wand; it complements the hard work and dedication you already invested in your training. Use it alongside your physical efforts, allowing both to fuel each other. Visualize yourself executing drills perfectly, strategizing on the fly, and triumphing in matches. This dual approach ensures that while your body hones its skills, your mind sharpens its focus.

So, take a few minutes each day to close your eyes and picture your success. Engage all your senses, feel the emotions, and immerse yourself in the experience. See yourself overcoming obstacles, reacting swiftly to challenges, and reaching your goals. By doing this consistently, you'll find that your performance on the field improves, your confidence grows, and your path to success becomes clearer.

Wrap it Up!

Alright, that's a wrap on how to use visualization to boost your game. We've covered the magic of mental rehearsal, where you fine-tune your skills without even stepping on the field. You now know how seeing yourself nailing those goals and making perfect passes can amp up your confidence levels like never before. Not to mention, focusing on your objectives and blocking out distractions becomes as easy as pie when you're mentally prepared.

So, whether you're dreaming about your next big match or just trying to improve your dribbling skills, remember that visualization is your secret weapon. It's all about creating vivid mental images, involving all your senses, and doing it consistently. With these techniques in your toolkit, you'll be ready to face any challenge head-on and play your best game every time. Happy visualizing, and go score some epic goals!

Maintaining a healthy lifestyle is all about making choices that support your goals both on and off the field. Whether you're snacking smart, getting enough sleep, or managing your time to juggle soccer and school, every decision you make helps shape your athletic performance and overall well-being. Let's explore this more in the next chapter.

Maintaining a Healthy Lifestyle

You owe it to yourself to be the best you can be.
–Christian Pulisic

Jake stood on the soccer field, feeling the sun warm his face as he watched his teammates practice shooting drills. He remembered the moment he decided to make a change in his life. Struggling with his performance and feeling tired all the time, he knew something had to give. One day, after a particularly disappointing game, he approached his coach, Mrs. Carter, ready to discuss his struggles. "I think I need help with my nutrition and recovery. Everything feels off," he said, nervously rubbing the back of his neck.

Mrs. Carter smiled knowingly. "It's great you recognize that, Jake. Soccer isn't just about skills on the field; it's also about how you care for your body. Let's work together on a plan." They sat down, and she explained the importance of a balanced diet and adequate sleep. Each word resonated with Jake as he took notes, feeling empowered to make real changes.

You might think it's all about those new cleats or the latest training drills, but the truth is, your performance starts way before you step onto the pitch. It's in the food you eat, the rest you get, and even how you balance your commitments. So, if you're looking to boost your game, it's time to dive into the nitty-gritty of what keeps you running at top speed.

In this chapter, we're going deep into the key aspects of maintaining a healthy lifestyle that supports your athletic dreams. We'll kick things off with some essential nutrition tips that will have you eating like a champion. Then, we'll explore the importance of sleep and recovery—because even superheroes need their downtime. Finally, we'll tackle the tricky topic of balancing your schoolwork, soccer practice, and personal life without losing your mind. Buckle up because we're here to help you become the best version of yourself, both on and off the field.

Nutrition Tips for Young Athletes

Look-we get it. Nutrition "advice" is everywhere! If you look on the internet, you might hear that ten different "diets" are all the BEST. It's so confusing! To get through all the noise, some simple concepts work great for most young athletes. Of course, there are people with allergies or personal beliefs about certain foods, which is cool. If you're one of those athletes, make sure you check with your parents or speak with your doctor if there's anything you're unsure about. For now, we're going to focus on what works for MOST people! Alright, let's dive in. Whether you're sprinting down the field or strategically planning your next move, what you eat plays a huge role in how well you perform. So, here's the lowdown on keeping your nutrition game strong.

Understanding the Basics of a Balanced Diet

First off, understanding the basics of a balanced diet is crucial. A balanced diet includes several components, including carbohydrates, proteins, and fats. These three nutrients are known as macronutrients, and they're vital for maintaining your energy levels and supporting overall health. When you think about what to include in your meals, it's helpful to recognize how each of these macronutrients plays a unique role in your body.

Carbohydrates: The Energy Source

Carbohydrates are your primary source of energy. They serve as the fuel that powers your day-to-day activities and workouts. Think of them as the gasoline you put in your car; without them, you won't get very far. When you consume carbohydrates, your body breaks them down into glucose, which is then used by your muscles and brain for energy.

Good sources of carbohydrates include whole grains such as brown rice and oatmeal. These foods provide not only energy but also dietary fiber, which is important for digestive health. Fruits and vegetables are also excellent carb sources. For example, bananas are a great snack before a workout because they provide quick energy. On the other hand, it's wise to limit your intake of sugary treats like cookies, candies, and soft drinks. These items may give you a quick burst of energy but often lead to a sugar crash later, leaving you feeling tired and sluggish.

Lionel Messi is all about balance. He enjoys pasta and rice, especially before a game. It's like he knows carbs are important for stamina but keeps it simple with wholesome options. Messi even loves a good pizza! It shows that consistency is key, but you can still enjoy your favorite foods.

Proteins: Building Blocks of Muscle

Proteins are up next, and they are vital for muscle repair and growth. Proteins are made up of smaller units called amino acids, which your body uses to build and repair tissues. After intense physical activity, your muscles go through wear and tear; consuming protein helps them heal and regain strength.

Lean meats such as chicken and turkey, fish, and low-fat dairy products like yogurt and cheese are excellent protein sources. If you are unable to eat certain meat, consider incorporating beans, lentils, and tofu into your meals. For example, a simple post-workout meal could be grilled chicken with quinoa and a side of steamed broccoli. This combination not only helps with muscle recovery but also provides essential vitamins and minerals needed for overall health.

Cristiano Ronaldo focuses on lean proteins like chicken and fish for muscle recovery. He also incorporates lots of fruits and vegetables in his meals. He often snacks on nuts for that healthy fat boost.

Fats: Essential for Energy

Last but not least, healthy fats are important for providing long-lasting energy. Fats are more calorie-dense than carbohydrates or proteins, so they can provide a significant amount of energy with a smaller serving. Additionally, fats play a role in absorbing fat-soluble vitamins (A, D, E, and K) and are essential for hormone production.

Healthy fats can be found in foods like avocados, nuts, seeds, and olive oil. For instance, adding a few slices of avocado to your toast or including a handful of nuts as a snack can enhance your meals. These sources of fats not only promote satiety but also offer various health benefits, including supporting heart health and reducing inflammation.

A balanced diet is about making informed choices and understanding the value of carbohydrates, proteins, and fats. Each of these nutrients plays a vital role in your health and wellness, and being mindful of what you eat can help you feel your best. Start small, making slow changes as you go, and make sure you enjoy your journey toward a healthier lifestyle.

Pre-Game Nutrition

What you eat before a game can set the stage for your performance. A meal rich in carbohydrates should be consumed 3–4 hours before the game. This gives you enough time to digest and helps you avoid feeling sluggish. Add moderate protein for muscle maintenance and keep it low in fat to ease digestion. Think pasta with marinara sauce, grilled chicken, and steamed veggies.

Timing is key here, too. About 45 minutes to an hour before the game, go for a lighter snack. This could be something like a banana, a small smoothie, or a handful of trail mix. The goal is to provide quick energy without weighing you down.

Speaking of pre-game nutrition, have you ever wondered what professionals eat before hitting the field? Kylian Mbappe sticks to a pre-game routine that involves consuming a good mix of protein and carbohydrates. Carbs give him the immediate energy boost he needs, while protein helps sustain that energy throughout the match. He specifically chooses foods like chicken, pasta, and fresh fruit a few hours before playing. Mbappe is so good at sticking to this routine that he's also able to enjoy his favorite indulgent dish, pasta carbonara!

Snack Smart

Snacking smart is a lifesaver both before and after games. For a quick energy boost, choose snacks like fruit, yogurt, or energy bars that are low in added sugars. Reading labels can help you make healthier choices. Look out for hidden sugars and opt for snacks that offer a good balance of nutrients.

After the game, snacking becomes even more important for recovery. A combination of protein and carbohydrates is ideal. Something simple like a peanut butter sandwich or yogurt with fruit can do wonders for muscle repair and replenishing energy stores (Purcell, 2013).

Post-Game Recovery Foods

Speaking of recovery, let's break down what you should eat post-game. Within 30 minutes to an hour after the game, aim to consume foods rich in protein to aid muscle repair. Carbohydrates are also crucial to reloading your energy levels. Think of a balanced meal like grilled chicken with quinoa and roasted veggies.

Electrolytes play a significant role in recovery by helping replace the fluids you've lost through sweat and maintaining fluid balance. Foods like bananas, oranges, and spinach can help restore these vital nutrients. If you're looking for a simple recipe, how about a smoothie with spinach, bananas, and some Greek yogurt? It's tasty and packed with nutrients.

> **Fun Fact:**
>
> Alex Morgan scored the game-winning goal in the 123rd minute of the 2012 Olympic semifinal against Canada, sending the U.S. to the final, where they won gold!
>
> *Did you know?*
>
> Alex Morgan is a huge fan of The Simpsons and was featured as a guest star in an episode where she played herself!

The Importance of Sleep and Recovery

When it comes to being a top-notch soccer player, sleep and recovery are often overshadowed by flashy goals and intense training sessions. But here's the kicker: Without proper rest, all your hard work on the field could go down the drain. Let's dive into why sleep and recovery are so crucial for athletic success and overall development.

Sleep Basics

First off, let's talk about how much sleep you need. For young athletes, it's generally recommended to get about 9 to 10 hours of sleep a night. Yeah, that might sound like a lot, especially when you've got school, homework, and maybe even chores to juggle. But your body needs time to rest so it can repair and grow stronger.

So, why does sleep matter so much? Well, sleep is like hitting the reset button on your body and mind. It's during sleep that your body produces growth hormone, which is essential for muscle repair and overall development (Fry & Rehman, 2021). Without enough sleep, you'll not only feel tired but also struggle to focus and perform well both on and off the field. Sleep deprivation can make you moody and less able to concentrate, turning you from a goal-scoring machine into a grumpy zombie.

Creating a Sleep-Friendly Environment

To maximize those precious Z's, it's essential to create a sleep-friendly environment. Start with your bedroom. It should be cool, dark, and quiet—a perfect cave for hibernation. You've probably heard this before, but it's really important to limit screen time before bed. Those late-night TikToks and Fortnite marathons might seem harmless, but the blue light from screens can mess up your melatonin production. Melatonin is the hormone that tells your brain it's time to sleep.

Instead of scrolling on your phone before bed, try establishing a calming bedtime routine. This could include reading a book, listening to some chill music, or even doing some light stretches. Anything that helps you wind down and signals to your body that it's time to sleep will do the trick.

Recovery Techniques

Now, let's chat about recovery techniques. While nutrition plays a huge role in recovery, there are several non-nutritional methods to help your body bounce back.

Stretching

Stretching is one of the simplest yet most effective ways. It helps enhance flexibility and keeps those muscles loose and ready for action. Try dedicating just 10 minutes after practice to stretch out your hamstrings, quads, and calves. Your future self will thank you.

Active Recovery

This involves low-intensity exercises like walking, swimming, or light jogging, designed to keep your blood flowing without putting too much strain on your muscles. Think of it as giving your body a gentle nudge rather than a full-on workout. Active recovery days are perfect after an intense game or practice session.

Rest Days

Then, there are rest days—complete days off from training. These are vital for muscle growth and overall recovery, allowing your body to heal any small injuries or strains you might not even be aware of.

Signs of Burnout

Recognizing signs of burnout is crucial for maintaining long-term success and well-being. Burnout isn't just physical; it's mental, too. If you're feeling constantly tired, easily irritated, or just not excited about playing soccer anymore, these could be signs that you need more recovery time. Physical indicators can include:

- persistent muscle soreness,
- frequent injuries,
- or even changes in appetite.

Open discussions with your coaches and parents are vital. They can't help you if they don't know what you're going through. Be honest about your feelings and symptoms.

Preventive measures include:

- setting realistic training goals,
- ensuring adequate rest periods,
- and making time for hobbies and activities outside of soccer.

A balanced approach to life will keep you healthier and happier in the long run.

Balancing School, Soccer, and Personal Life

Managing academic responsibilities alongside soccer commitments can be challenging, but with the right strategies, it's achievable. Let's dive into some practical tips to help you balance both effectively and avoid feeling overwhelmed.

Using Your Time Wisely

First things first: Mastering time management is crucial. Start by creating a schedule that includes all your commitments. Planners and calendar apps are lifesavers here! Block out specific times for studying, attending classes, practicing, and even downtime. Remember that being consistent with your schedule helps you form a routine, making it easier to stick to your plans.

Something you can try is to review your schedule weekly. Look at what's coming up and adjust as needed. This ensures you're always prepared, whether it's for an upcoming game or a big exam.

To bring it closer to home, let's look at young athletes balancing multiple life commitments. Take Sam, a high school soccer player who juggles practice, games, and academics. Using time management techniques, Sam creates a schedule that allocates specific times for studying, training, and social activities. He uses a planner to ensure he doesn't miss any deadlines or practices.

Sam also communicates openly with his parents and coach about his commitments. When his academic load increases, he informs his coach, who then adjusts his training schedule accordingly. This balance allows Sam to excel both on the field and in the classroom. It's not just about managing time but also about setting priorities and knowing when to seek help.

Setting Priorities

With so many responsibilities, it's essential to learn how to prioritize. Not all tasks are created equal; some need immediate attention, while others can wait. Make a list of what needs to be done each day and rank them by importance. For example, if you have a major test and a soccer match on the same day, create a study plan that allows you to prepare without sacrificing your athletic performance.

Balancing your short-term responsibilities along with your long-term goals is another important aspect. While daily tasks are important, keep an eye on larger objectives like improving your grades over the semester or enhancing your skills for the season. Break these long-term goals into smaller, manageable steps to keep track of your progress.

Personal Time and Well-Being

Maintaining personal time and well-being is just as important as managing academics and athletics. Downtime isn't optional; it's necessary for mental health. Schedule breaks between studies and practices to recharge. This could be as simple as a walk or some quiet reading time.

Engaging in activities outside of soccer can also be refreshing. Hobbies and interests help develop a well-rounded personality and offer a much-needed break from the routine grind. Whether it's painting, playing a musical instrument, or joining a club at school, these activities provide a creative outlet and reduce stress.

Remember, your well-being directly impacts both your academic and athletic performances. It's not about doing more; it's about doing things smartly and taking care of yourself along the way.

Mia is an inspiring young athlete who balances her love for soccer with personal activities. Mia finds time for hobbies outside soccer, such as painting and reading. This downtime helps her maintain mental well-being and prevents burnout. She's learned the importance of taking breaks and enjoys activities that allow her to relax and recharge.

It's possible to excel in sports while maintaining other aspects of life. It takes effective time management, clear communication, and understanding the value of rest and recovery to strike a balance. So, whether you're aspiring to be the next big soccer star or simply enjoying the sport, these strategies can help you maintain a healthy lifestyle that boosts your performance.

Wrap it Up!

Alright, folks, as we wrap up this chapter, remember that creating a healthy lifestyle is your secret weapon to becoming a top-notch soccer player. We've tackled the basics of balanced nutrition, pre-game meals that won't leave you feeling like a sluggish potato, and smart snacking habits. We also broke down why sleep is more than just a luxury—it's a necessity for keeping you sharp and focused on and off the field. Throw in some recovery techniques like stretching and active recovery, and you're well on your way to being unstoppable.

But hey, life isn't all about soccer, right? Balancing school, personal life, and training can be a juggling act worthy of a circus performer. Yet, with solid time management, setting priorities, and communicating with your coaches and parents, it's doable. So go ahead, fuel up properly, get those precious Z's, and make sure to carve out some time for fun activities outside soccer. Remember, it's about performing your best while living your best life. Now, let's put these tips into action and watch you shine!

---

*If this playbook inspired you, we'd love to hear your thoughts—please leave a review and help others discover the power of mental toughness!

Conclusion

Alright, team, we've reached the end of our playbook. Before you scoot off to conquer the soccer world, let's huddle up for a quick recap and some final words to fuel that fire in your belly.

So, what have we learned? First off, mental toughness isn't just a fancy term; it's your secret weapon on the field. We've dug into a lot: setting those SMART goals to keep you focused, finding your motivation when Netflix calls your name louder than your soccer coach, and building resilience to bounce back from any setback.

Remember how we talked about SMART goals? Specific, measurable, achievable, relevant, time-bound—it's not just an acronym but a strategy. If Mia Hamm could do it, you can too. Whether it's nailing that perfect penalty kick or mastering a new dribble, setting clear goals keeps your eyes on the prize. And let's be real, crossing items off a list is super satisfying.

Resilience is not just about surviving life's challenges; it's about thriving because of them. It's about staying in the game even when things get tough. So when you're on the field, keep fighting, keep pushing. Let your heart guide you and your mind reinforce that you can and will bounce back. Carry this mindset with you, not just in soccer but in all walks of life, for you are tougher than you think. You have the power to shine brightly, even in the face of adversity.

Take a moment to reflect on your heroes. Influential players— those whose journeys you admire—often have resilience woven deeply into their stories. Maybe it's a player like Alex Morgan. Before she became a star, she faced numerous rejections and injuries. But she kept pushing. Each time she felt the weight of disappointment, she turned that into fuel, channeling it back onto the field. When you face your obstacles, remember why you started playing in the first place. It wasn't just about winning games; it was about your love for the sport, the bonds made with teammates, and the challenge of improving. Let that passion be the fire that strengthens your resilience.

Motivation, motivation, motivation. It's like trying to find the lost civilization of Atlantis sometimes, but look at it this way: Every time you lace up your boots or decide to practice instead of binge-watching that new show, you're investing in yourself. You're closer to being the player who stands tall, rain or shine, loss or victory. Find what fires you up. Maybe it's imagining yourself scoring the winning goal in a championship game or simply wanting to beat your own personal best. Keep that image front and center, and let it drive you.

And then there's resilience—bouncing back after life tackles you hard. We all know those moments: missed opportunities, lost matches, or even injuries. But hey, Cristiano Ronaldo didn't become CR7 without facing some brutal tackles along the way. It's okay to feel down momentarily, but what makes champions stand out is their ability to rise. Each time you get back up, you're mentally stronger. Think of setbacks as just another opponent to outplay.

Now, here's the thing: Your journey doesn't end with this book. Nope, getting mentally tough is like leveling up in a video game— there's always more to learn and achieve. You've got the basics now, but keep practicing them. Every training session and every match is another chance to build on these skills. Embrace every challenge that comes your way and see it as an opportunity to grow. Growth isn't instant; it's a continuous process, like learning to juggle or executing that perfect bicycle kick. Practice, patience, and persistence—the three P's of mental toughness.

And here's one last nugget of wisdom: Remember that mental toughness isn't just for the soccer field. The lessons you've learned can help you tackle school projects, deal with friendship drama, or push through any challenges life throws your way. Being strong-minded isn't just about sports; it's about living your best life.

When you step onto the field or face any challenge in life, remember that it's all about making the effort to be your best self.

You've got this. Go out there, give it your all, and remember every little step counts. Now go make us proud!

Looking for a short playbook while on the go? See the original introduction to this series, "Mind over Matter: A Mental Toughness Playbook for Young Athletes"—designed to sharpen your skills in any sport!

https://mybook.to/UzRlWS

References

ActiveCollab Team. (2023, April 21). *What is team dynamics? Importance, key elements, and factors.* ActiveCollab. https://activecollab.com/blog/collaboration/team-dynamics

Adams, A. J. (2009, December 3). *Seeing is believing: The power of visualization.* Psychology Today. https://www.psychologytoday.com/us/blog/flourish/200912/seeing-is-believing-the-power-visualization

Admin. (2020, March 4). *Dispelling myths about mental toughness.* Caelin White Psychologist. https://www.caelinwhitepsychologist.com/index.php/2016/05/31/mental-toughness/

Anonymous. (n.d.). Quote. In Goodbye Self Help (2022), *45+ inspirational soccer quotes to help you play your best.* Goodbye Self Help. https://www.goodbyeselfhelp.com/inspirational-soccer-quotes/

Ashdown, B., Sarkar, M., Saward, C., & Johnston, J. (2024). Exploring the behavioral indicators of resilience in professional academy youth soccer. *Journal of Applied Sport Psychology; Taylor & Francis.* https://doi.org/10.1080/10413200.2024.2361701

Balancing academics and athletics: Tips for college sports success. (n.d.). Marygrove College Athletics. https://www.marygrovemustangs.com/balancing-academics-and-athletics-tips-for-college-sports-success.html

Brar, R. (2018, May 1). *How LeBron cheats father time.* Medium. https://medium.com/grandstandcentral/lebron-james-health-and-fitness-regime-279804adb749

Buck, M. (2023, October 20). *20 Mindfulness exercises for athletes.* Athlete Mental Health. https://purposesoulathletics.com/20-mindfulness-exercises-for-athletes/

Calandrino, A. (2024, August 5). *The power of visualization in achieving your goals.* Amy Calandrino.

https://www.amycalandrino.com/mindsetmakeover/the-power-of-visualization-in-achieving-your-goals

Clarey, C. (2014, February 22). Olympians use imagery as mental training. *The New York Times.* https://www.nytimes.com/2014/02/23/sports/olympics/olympi ans-use-imagery-as-mental-training.html

Crimmins, J. (2023, May 30). *How to develop the power of visualization in sports performance.* The Behaviour Institute. https://thebehaviourinstitute.com/how-to-develop-the-power-of-visualization-in-sports-performance/

Dagmar. (2024, April 25). *The best nutrition tips for young athletes on game day.* Peace of Mind Insurance. https://www.getpomi.com/nutrition-tips-young-athletes-game-day/

Dailyhuman. (2023, November 29). *Dynamic team building activities for youth sports teams: A Coach's Toolkit.* Dailyhuman. https://www.dailyhuman.com/post/sports-team-building-activities

Daily visualization practices for manifesting your goals. (2024, April 15). Warriors of the Divine. https://warriorsdivine.com/blogs/the-path/daily-visualization-practices-for-manifesting-your-goals?srsltid=AfmBOopvtlCH3dPdK67ibspZs6J4h1tdc8mKi QmTwIxzXxwD8Ufslb1U

David. (2024, July 24). *Psychology for soccer players.* Elite Football Coaching Sydney. https://elitefootballcoaching.com.au/psychology-for-soccer-players/

Fadare, S. A., Lambaco, E., Mangorsi, Y. B., Lorchano, J. D. L., & Juvenmile, T. B. (2022). A voyage into the visualization of athletic performances: A review. *American Journal of Multidisciplinary Research and Innovation, 1*(3), 105-109. https://doi.org/10.54536/ajmri.v1i3.479

Farris, S. (2024, July 8). *Athletes & mental health: Misconceptions and stigma.* Anxiety in Athletes. https://anxietyinathletes.org/athletes/talking-about-anxiety-and-ocd/misconceptions-and-stigma/

Ferguson, A. (n.d.). *Alex Ferguson quotes*. Goodreads. https://www.goodreads.com/quotes/891120-i-had-to-lift-players-expectations-they-should-never-give

Fry, A., & Rehman, A. (2023, December 13). *Sleep, athletic performance, and recovery*. Sleep foundation. https://www.sleepfoundation.org/physical-activity/athletic-performance-and-sleep

Gormaz, P. (2022, May 4). *The secrets to dominating in your sport PART 3 – pressure*. Neurotracker. https://www.neurotrackerx.com/post/the-secrets-to-dominating-in-your-sport-part-3-pressure

Hamm, M. (n.d.-a). *Mia Hamm quotes*. BrainyQuote. https://www.brainyquote.com/quotes/mia_hamm_204528

Hamm, M. (n.d.-b). *Mia Hamm quotes*. Quotefancy. https://quotefancy.com/quote/1223398/Mia-Hamm-Every-single-day-I-wake-up-and-commit-myself-to-becoming-a-better-player-Some

Henriksen, K. (2022). *The magic of mindfulness in sport*. Frontiers for Young Minds. https://doi.org/10.3389/frym.2022.683827

Henry, T. (n.d.). Quote. In parklandsoccer (2024), *"I always believed in pushing myself to be the best I could be, and that hard work and determination would* [Image attached]. Instagram. https://www.instagram.com/parklandsoccer/p/C3jhGQXtV7V/?img_index=1

How does sleep impact athletic performance? (n.d.). Children's Hospital Colorado. https://www.childrenscolorado.org/conditions-and-advice/sports-articles/sports-safety/sleep-student-athletes-performance/

How to turn self-doubt into confidence. (2024, January 18). Peak Performance Sports. https://www.peaksports.com/sports-psychology-blog/how-to-turn-self-doubt-into-confidence/

Ireland, J. (2023, February 20). *The three key pieces to building mental toughness in soccer*. Expand Your Game. https://expandyourgame.com/mental-toughness-in-soccer/

Kylian Mbappé news. (n.d.). IMDb. https://www.imdb.com/name/nm9072528/news/

Lapchick, R. (2020, February 19). *Lapchick: Racism reported in sports decreasing but still prevalent.* ESPN. https://www.espn.com/espn/story//id/28738336/racism-reported-sports-decreasing-prevalent

Latinjak, A. T., & Hatzigeorgiadis, A. (2022, April 7). *Self-talk: Chats that athletes have with themselves. Frontiers for Young Minds.* https://doi.org/10.3389/frym.2022.681923

A look inside: Daily routines of professional baseball players. (n.d.). Marygrove College Athletics. https://www.marygrovemustangs.com/a-look-inside-daily-routines-of-professional-baseball-players.html

Martín-Rodríguez, A., Gostian-Ropotin, L. A., Beltrán-Velasco, A. I., Belando-Pedreño, N., Simón, J. A., López-Mora, C., Navarro-Jiménez, E., Tornero-Aguilera, J. F., & Clemente-Suárez, V. J. (2024). Sporting mind: The interplay of physical activity and psychological health. *Sports, 12*(1), 37. https://doi.org/10.3390/sports12010037

Maslen, P. (2015, December 29). The Social and Academic Benefits of Team Sports. Edutopia; George Lucas Educational Foundation. https://www.edutopia.org/discussion/social-and-academic-benefits-team-sports

May, K. (2012, October 1). *Some examples of how power posing can boost your confidence. TED Blog* https://blog.ted.com/10-examples-of-how-power-posing-can-work-to-boost-your-confidence/

Media. (2022, December 13). *Strategies and methods of improving motivation for athletes and fitness clients.* National Exercise and Sports Trainers Association. https://www.nestacertified.com/strategies-and-methods-of-improving-motivation-for-athletes-and-fitness-clients/

Messi, L. (n.d.). *Lionel Messi quotes.* BrainyQuote. https://www.brainyquote.com/quotes/lionel_messi_473554

Metrifit. (2021, March 16). *The importance of goal setting for athletes.* Metrifit. https://metrifit.com/blog/the-importance-of-goal-setting-for-athletes/

Morgan, A. (n.d.). Quote. In Goodbye Self Help (2022), *45+ inspirational soccer quotes to help you play your best.* Goodbye Self Help.

https://www.goodbyeselfhelp.com/inspirational-soccer-quotes/

Mourinho, J. (n.d.). Quote. In Coachbetter (2024), *"The most important quality a player can have is not skill, but mentality"* [Image attached]. Twitter. https://twitter.com/CoachBetter_ltd/status/1749753596730564896

Nath, M., Singh, V., & Mishra, A. (2022). Mental toughness among national soccer officials: A comparative analysis. *Journal of Public Health in Africa.* https://doi.org/10.4081/jphia.2022.2423

Norris, G., & Norris, H. (2021, July 15). *Building resilience through sport in young people with adverse childhood experiences.* Frontiers in Sports and Active Living. https://doi.org/10.3389/fspor.2021.663587

Perrey, S. (2022). Training monitoring in sports: It Is time to embrace cognitive demand. *Sports, 10*(4), 56. https://doi.org/10.3390/sports10040056

Persaud, R. (2022, November 30). *Cognitive strategies of elite soccer players and athletes.* Psychology Today. https://www.psychologytoday.com/us/blog/slightly-blighty/202211/cognitive-strategies-elite-soccer-players-and-athletes?msockid=04ebe4c2f2246d453f6cf7cbf3076c25

Petiot, G. H., Bagatin, R., Aquino, R., & Raab, M. (2021). Key characteristics of decision making in soccer and their implications. *New Ideas in Psychology, 61*(0732-118X), 100846. https://doi.org/10.1016/j.newideapsych.2020.100846

The psychology of weightlifting: Building mental resilience. (2024, April 2). USA Weightlifting. https://www.usaweightlifting.org/news/2024/april/01/the-psychology-of-weightlifting-building-mental-resilience

Pulisic, C. (n.d.). Quote. In Soccer.com (2020), *Words of wisdom for the weekend, courtesy of Christian Pulisic* [Image]. Facebook. https://www.facebook.com/soccerdotcom/photos/words-of-wisdom-for-the-weekend-courtesy-of-christian-pulisic-tag-a-friend-or-te/10157221885436463/

Purcell, L. K. (2013). Sports nutrition for young athletes. *Paediatrics & Child Health, 18*(4), 200–205. https://doi.org/10.1093/pch/18.4.200

Richardson, M. (2023, October 19). *The power of positive psychology: Building resilience in young athletes.* Legacy Pro Sports. https://legacyprosports.us/the-power-of-positive-psychology-building-resilience-in-young-athletes/

Robinson, E. (2024, April 16). *SMART goals.* Mental Training Plan. https://www.mentaltrainingplan.com/post/smart-goals

Saidon, N. (2024, April 25). *How to help athletes with failure.* Balance Is Better. https://balanceisbetter.org.nz/how-to-help-athletes-with-failure/

Selby. (2023, August 21).*Building character on the field: Fun and effective sportsmanship teaching activities.* Everyday Speech. https://everydayspeech.com/blog-posts/general/building-character-on-the-field-fun-and-effective-sportsmanship-teaching-activities/

The Socratic Method (2024, January 22). *John Wooden: 'success is peace of mind, which is a direct result of self-satisfaction in knowing you made the effort to become the best of which you are capable.'* The Socratic Method. https://www.socratic-method.com/quote-meanings-and-interpretations/john-wooden-success-is-peace-of-mind-which-is-a-direct-result-of-self-satisfaction-in-knowing-you-made-the-effort-to-become-the-best-of-which-you-are-capable

Sports Hawgs. (2024, August 13). *Cultivating mental toughness in athletes: Beyond the physical training.* Sports Hawgs. https://sportshawgs.com/blogs/news/cultivating-mental-toughness-in-athletes-beyone-the-physical-training?srsltid=AfmBOopAIZPzWyV_3dWosP1LViKvbviGWXyqJUyc-4iFF7MP23uQQvzG

Sports visualization: The secret weapon of athletes. (2024, January 22). Peak Performance Sports. https://www.peaksports.com/sports-psychology-blog/sports-visualization-athletes/

SuccessMatters4me. (2023, June 7). *Short motivational stories for athletes: Inspiring performance and building resilience.* Medium. https://successmatters4me.medium.com/short-motivational-stories-for-athletes-inspiring-performance-and-building-resilience-62d11f7934e4

Sutton, J. (2024, April 1). *Boosting mental toughness in young athletes & 20 Strategies.* PositivePsychology.com. https://positivepsychology.com/mental-toughness-for-young-athletes/

10 Inspiring examples of highly resilient sportspeople. (2023, May 9). Resilience Institute. https://resiliencei.com/blog/10-inspiring-examples-of-highly-resilient-sportspeople

Tred, K. (2023, October 28). *The power of visualization in achieving success: Harnessing the mind-body connection.* Medium. https://medium.com/@tredkev/the-power-of-visualization-in-achieving-success-harnessing-the-mind-body-connection-d26673bcc962

Wang, Y., Lei, S.-M., & Fan, J. (2023, January 22). Effects of mindfulness-based interventions on promoting athletic performance and related factors among athletes: A systematic review and Meta-analysis of randomized controlled trial. *International Journal of Environmental Research and Public Health.* https://doi.org/10.3390/ijerph20032038

Ways to help teen athletes through mistakes and losses. (2022, January 11). Children's Mercy. https://www.childrensmercy.org/parent-ish/2022/01/mistakes-and-losses/

Wieser, R., & Thiel, H. (2014). A survey of "mental hardiness" and "mental toughness" in professional male football players. *Chiropractic & Manual Therapies*, *22*(1). https://doi.org/10.1186/2045-709x-22-17

Wilson, L. (2019, March 4). *Positive self-talk for your athletes.* Coaches Toolbox. https://www.coachestoolbox.net/mental-toughness/positive-self-talk-for-your-athletes

Wooden, J. (n.d.). *John Woden quotes.* BrainyQuote. https://www.brainyquote.com/quotes/john_wooden_402561

Printed in Dunstable, United Kingdom

73667433R00078